THE RIGH
TO DO WRONG

AN EXPOSE OF SUCCESSFUL CRIMINALS

BY
HARRY HOUDINI

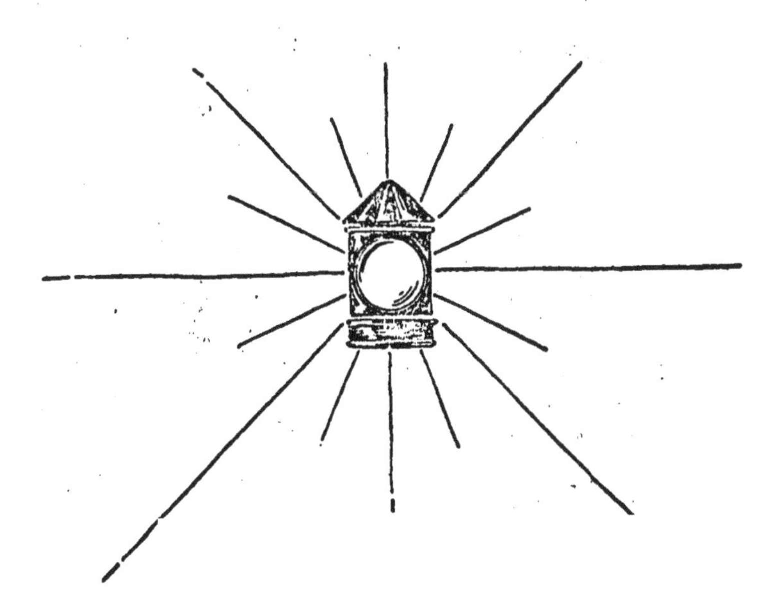

PHOTO BY J. FLEMING, CHICAGO

HARRY HOUDINI

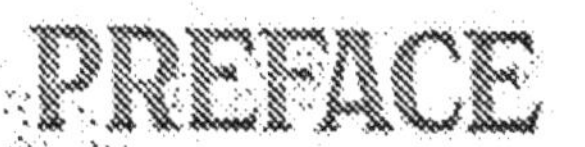

> O would the deed were good!
> For now the Devil, that told me I did well,
> Says that this deed is chronicled in Hell!
> — *Shakespeare.*

THERE is an under world — a world of cheat and crime — a world whose highest good is successful evasion of the laws of the land.

You who live your life in placid respectability know but little of the real life of the denizens of this world. The daily records of the police courts, the startling disclosures of fraud and swindle in newspaper stories are about all the public know of this world of crime. Of the real thoughts and feelings of the criminal, of the terrible fascination which binds him to his nefarious career, of the thousands — yea, tens of thousands — of undiscovered crimes and unpunished criminals, you know but little.

The object of this book is twofold: First, to safeguard the public against the practises of the criminal classes by exposing their various tricks and explaining the adroit methods by which they seek to defraud. "Knowledge is power" is an old saying. I might paraphrase it in this case by saying knowledge is safety. I wish to put the public on its guard, so that honest folks may be able to detect and protect themselves from the dishonest, who labor under the false impression that it is easier to live dishonestly than to thrive by honest means.

In the second place, I trust this book will afford entertaining, as well as instructive reading, and that the facts and experiences, the exposés and explanations here set forth may serve to interest you, as well as put you in a position where you will be less liable to fall a victim.

The material contained in this book has been collected by me personally during many years of my active professional life. It has been my good fortune to meet personally and converse with the chiefs of police and the most famous detectives in all the great cities of the world. To these gentlemen I am indebted for many amusing and instructive incidents hitherto unknown to the world.

The work of collecting and arranging this material and writing the different chapters has occupied many a leisure hour. My only wish is that "The Right Way to Do Wrong" may amuse and entertain my readers and place the unwary on their guard. If my humble efforts in collecting and writing these facts shall accomplish this purpose, I shall be amply repaid, and feel that my labor has not been in vain.

HARRY HOUDINI,
Handcuff King and Jail Breaker.

THE FOX, THE GREATEST THIEF IN THE WORLD

CONTENTS

SHOT ONE

INCOME OF A CRIMINAL

PEOPLE of respectability and inexperience, who have no knowledge of the criminal classes, usually imagine that every criminal is a hardened villain, incapable of even the ordinary feelings of family affection, and that of necessity the professional crook, thief, or burglar is uneducated and ignorant.

In fact, nothing could be more remote from the truth. Do you see that well-dressed, respectable-looking man glancing over the editorial page of the *Sun?* You would be surprised to know that he is a professional burglar and that he has a loving wife and a family of children who little know the "business" which takes him away for many days and nights at a time!

You meet a grave and benevolent-looking gentleman on a railway train; perhaps he shares your seat and interests you by his brilliant and intelligent conversation. You little suspect that he is at the head of a gang of the most expert bank burglars in the country!

As a matter of fact, some of the brightest brains and keenest minds belong to professional criminals. They live by their wits and must needs keep those wits sharp and active. Not that I would have you think that all professional criminals go about in the guise of gentlemen. There are all grades of culture and lack of culture in the various nefarious callings of crime. The sneak thief and the burglar may and often does look the "hard citizen" he is; but you will never find him lacking in a certain kind of quick wits and a certain kind

HOLD-UP MEN AT WORK

of brain power. So highly organized is the machinery of the law and police protection in our modern civilization that one of the first requisites for success as a professional criminal is brains.

Does It Pay to Commit Crime?

This is a question I have often asked the chiefs of police and great detectives of every country in the world. How great are the money rewards of evil doing? Does a "good" burglar have an income equal to that of a bank president? Can a pickpocket make more money than the fashionable tailor who makes the pockets? Is a gambler better paid than a governor? Can a shoplifter make more money than the saleswoman? In fact, does it pay to be a criminal, and, if so, how great is the reward for evil doing?

I am aware that it is the general impression, considered simply as a matter of profits, that the professional criminal is well paid. He gets something for nothing; therefore you would say at a first glance that he must be rolling in wealth.

Many people who get their ideas of criminals from novels and story papers, for instance, imagine a gambler as a man who always has a roll of bills in his pocket big enough to choke a horse, as they say. No doubt, also, the histories of sensational coups as reported in the daily press are chiefly responsible for this false impression. But such colossal frauds and robberies are rarely the work of professional criminals. They are usually perpetrated by men whose previous good character has placed them in positions of trust. Men who have led honest lives, when temptation came along and on paper they figured out that they could not lose — why, they stole and fell — into the clutches of the law. Disgraced, they are ruined for life, often ruining all their family. It is a terrible thing to have the finger of fate point at you with the remark, "His father is serving time for doing so and so," or "Her brother is now in his sixteenth year, and comes out in five years."

Such humble criminals as the area sneak thief, the porch and hallway thieves, and the ordinary shoplifter may be dismissed with a few words; their gains are miserably small, they live in abject poverty, and after detection (for sooner or later they are detected) they end their lives in the workhouse!

"If I could earn $5 a week honest, I'd gladly give up 'dragging' [shoplifting]," said a thief of this type to a New York detective; "but I can't stand regular work, never could; it's so much easier to 'prig' things." No avarice, but simple laziness keeps these thieves dishonest.

More lucrative are the callings of the counter thief, the pickpocket, and the "buzzer" or watch thief. Of those the pickpocket wins the largest returns. A purse hunter who knows his work would think he had wasted his time if he did not make $5 on an evening stroll. Race meetings and fairs may bring him in $100 to $150 a day, but an average day's makings amount to only $8 to $12.

AT THE PISTOL'S MUZZLE

The passing of bad money, as every one knows,

who is behind the scenes in criminal life, is a very poorly paid "industry," while the punishment risked is heavy. In England the "snide pitchers" or "shovers of the queer," as they were called, used to buy the counterfeit coins at so much a dozen, and, working in pairs, pass them out in shops.

Highwaymen, robbers, and hold-up men sometimes make big hauls, but their careers are short. Into their brutal hands pass many a diamond pin or ring, many a gold chain, worth $20 or $25, even at melting-pot prices of some dishonest goldsmith. Happily for society, these ruffians are speedily brought to book and their ill-gotten gains are dearly earned. There is a thieves' proverb which runs, "A six months' run and the hook (thief) is done." The garrote and hold-up men have far shorter lease of liberty and frequently fall into the clutches of the law within a day or two after release from prison.

Both burglars and confidence men may make big coups occasionally, but their income is precarious. The burglar is at the mercy of the "fence," as the receiver of stolen goods is called, and realizes only a small part of the actual value of his pelf. I suppose a burglar would be considered very successful if he made $3,000 a year actual profit. The "fence" has much larger opportunities and his voracity is well known. A detective friend was well acquainted with one who made as much as $5,000 a year for several years and finally shot himself to avoid arrest. Another "fence" actually amassed a fortune, but his wealth did not prevent him from dying miserably in prison.

The truth is, that a life of dishonesty may pay at first when you are not known to the police, but when an offender once falls into the hands of the ever-watchful police he begins to be a well-known customer. He now pays dearer and dearer every time he is brought up for trial. His brief spells of liberty are spent in committing some crime that once again brings him back to the prison, so when you figure out the sentences he has to serve, why, his honest gains are contemptible compared to such awful penalties.

As this book is not a history of crime or criminals, to those wishing to read positive facts of great criminals, and all of them have either died in the poorhouse or are yet counting the weary days in prison cells, divorced from wife, from children, and from all ties that human beings hold so dear, I can safely call attention to the book called "Our Rival the Rascal!" written by my friend Chief Inspector of Police, Wm. B. Watts, of Boston, Mass. This book is the greatest book on the subject that I have ever seen. I happened to have a copy with me in Berlin, when the royal police, hearing that I had the book in the country, asked me as a favor to allow them to make extracts and photograph some of the famous criminals in the book.

This I allowed them to do and in return they handed me several photos of well-known criminals to send to Chief Inspector, Wm. B. Watts. In order to put a finish to this chapter, it can be said that IT DOES NOT PAY TO LEAD A DISHONEST LIFE, and to those who read this book, although it will inform them "The Right Way to Do Wrong," all I have to say is one word and that is "DON'T."

"Yus, my poor brother had no eddication, and it wur his ruin!"

"How was that?"

"He forged a name on a check, an' the spellin' wur bad."

SHOT TWO

PROFESSIONAL BURGLARY

THE professional burglar is a man of resources and daring. He has usually had a long training in criminal pursuits. A good burglar is a man who knows how to keep his own counsel and is very careful how he tells his plans to any one else.

If the same amount of ability and talent that many a criminal exercises to become a professional burglar were applied to an honest pursuit, he would gain wealth and fame; but once started in the path of crime it is difficult to turn aside.

The burglar who makes the breaking into houses a profession is held by the fascination of the danger and the rewards of his pursuit. The consciousness that he is able to accomplish the almost impossible, to plan and bring off coups which fill the newspapers with flare headings, is as much a matter of pride to him as high attainments in an honorable profession are to another man.

Planning a Bold Break. When a burglar starts out on a job he does not do it haphazardly. He carefully selects a house in a favorable location, occupied by a family who are known to have valuable possessions worth taking away. The retired location of the house, the ease of access, every approach and every avenue of escape if detected are carefully studied. Then he goes about acquainting himself with the habits of the people who occupy the house. He soon knows when they come and go, how the doors are fastened, how the windows are secured. Perhaps he ingratiates himself by and ing marked attention to the cove ds of the kitchen, and so attr rns the inside workings of the thi ousehold. Usually this is accomplished by the aid of a confederate or member of the gang to which he belongs, and if he can induce the cooperation of some servant his work is made so much the easier.

A SOURCE OF INFORMATION

At length the night of the burglary arrives. The date has been carefully set. You may be sure that there is not a full moon to illuminate the grounds, as he has consulted the almanac. If there is a watch-dog, the burglar carries ample means to quiet him, in the shape of a small bottle of chloroform. Accompanied by his pal (for most of these burglars work in pairs) they rapidly effect their entrance in accordance with their plan. Usually one man is stationed outside, to give warning by means of a peculiar whistle or other sound in case detection is to be feared.

How the burglar overcomes all the obstacles of his entrance into the house will be treated later, but to a professional cracksman the ordinary locks of doors, the ordinary window fastenings and safety arrangements which the householder attends to so carefully every night offer but little or no obstacle. When the time comes for him to enter, he enters as quietly and quickly as though he were the master himself — in fact, very much more quietly. Once inside, his glimmering electric dark lantern, which can be hooded in an instant, gives him sufficient light to move with noiseless rubber-soled shoes to the different apartments. The absolute silence in which a professional cracksman can go through a house, avoiding creaking doors, and escaping every loose board which may betray his presence is aston ing. Many a householder has awakened in the morning find his house rifled who would deem it impossible for ai one to enter his house, much less his room, without immed. ately arousing him.

To show how carefully a burglar plans for the "cracking" of some specially desirable "crib," one ex-convict declares that he has often expended large sums of money in making the preliminary arrangements for some great coup. If a burglar should happen to be caught in the house-breaking act, it is fairly important that he should not be recognized afterwards; so most professional burglars are very careful to provide themselves with a disguise when out on their "work." One reformed criminal told Inspector Byrnes that he had several times been seen by people while entering houses, but they had never once been able to recognize him afterwards. His simple plan he described as follows: "I always wore a specially made wig, with false side-whiskers and moustache of the best quality. My wardrobe was extensive, and contained reversible coats and reversible trousers, after the style used by quick-change artists on the stage. With the aid of these, I have been able to make a complete change of appearance in less than two minutes." It is easy to see how rogues take more pains to perpetrate robberies than honest men do to get a living.

The Burglar Who Walked Backward. A London burglar, who served a long sentence, told the chaplain of the prison the following amusing story of one of his experiences: "One of the toughest pieces of work I undertook was a big jewelry shop in the Seven Sisters Road, one January night. It was a 'put up' job,—that is, the business came to me through one of the brokers who supply burglars with places for likely hauls, and receive in return a large commission. The jewelry store in this case was protected by iron shutters, not easy to open from the street, but valuable goods were supposed to be left over night in the window.

"I approached the crib down a narrow entry to the rear,

and along this I walked backward, for the ground was covered with snow, and any tracks going forward would attract the next policeman who should pass. I continued on this crab-like progress until under the shutter of the rear window. This I got through without difficulty, but was confronted by a door leading into the passage, which was locked. On attempting to force it with a jimmy, the door fell together with its case with a tremendous crash. I need not say I made myself scarce in a jiffy, and hid behind a shed in the yard. Strange to say, nothing happened. No one seemed to have heard the terrible racket. I re-entered, and, climbing to the top of the stairs, found a heavy trap-door fastened with a massive bolt. This gave way after a special treatment, and in the big sitting-room, by the glimmer of my tiny dark lantern, I found a few watches. The door leading into the shop was fastened with a mortise lock, and it was necessary to cut the box out. Much to my disgust, I found the show-window absolutely empty. In ransacking the place, I came across a small iron safe which, with a vast deal of trouble, I dragged into the basement, where I set to work with my safe-opening tools, feeling sure I should find my plunder, but again I was disappointed, for the safe was empty." (Almost all English safes are key-locked, not combination as in America.)

"Where was the stuff? Clearly the jeweler had some hiding-place. I resolved not to get 'cold feet' on this job, so went back to make a systematic search. Outside the old couple's bedroom, I listened carefully. All was quiet. I entered as silently as a shadow, and found the old jeweler and his wife sleeping soundly. A revolver was on the chair by his bedside. I have always considered the practise of keeping revolvers about the house most dangerous, especially to casual night visitors, so I pocketed this one, gathered up the loose money, two gold watches, and, turning, found arranged along the wall, the rods of jewelry and watches from the shop window. I selected as many as my pockets would hold, and cautiously made my way downstairs again. Upon leaving the house, I walked backward again through the snow, and almost collided with the milkman just starting on his rounds.

"'You have a very remarkable way of walking,' he said.

"'Oh,' I replied, 'it is an agreeable change after the monotony of always walking forward; but in the daytime I cannot practise it, owing to the remarks of foolish people who will not mind their own business.'

"He seemed to enter into the joke, but no sooner had we reached the road, than he shouted, 'Police!' and 'Stop thief!' for all he was worth.

"I had a good start, however, and two hours later a Hoxton 'fence' received a considerable addition to his store of valuables concealed under the floor of his bedroom."

The question has often been asked how burglars get away with their booty, especially when it makes, as it often does, a bulky bundle. The police are apt to be suspicious of people who carry bundles in the small hours of the night, and ask inconvenient questions. If any one doubts this, let him try the experiment of going out between two and three in the morning, carrying a bag heavily loaded with bricks. He will not proceed many yards without being pounced upon by a "cop." A story in point is told by an ex-convict to a well-known detective. "I had a pal with me, and we broke into the country palace of one of the wealthiest dukes in England. The silver-plate we got filled two

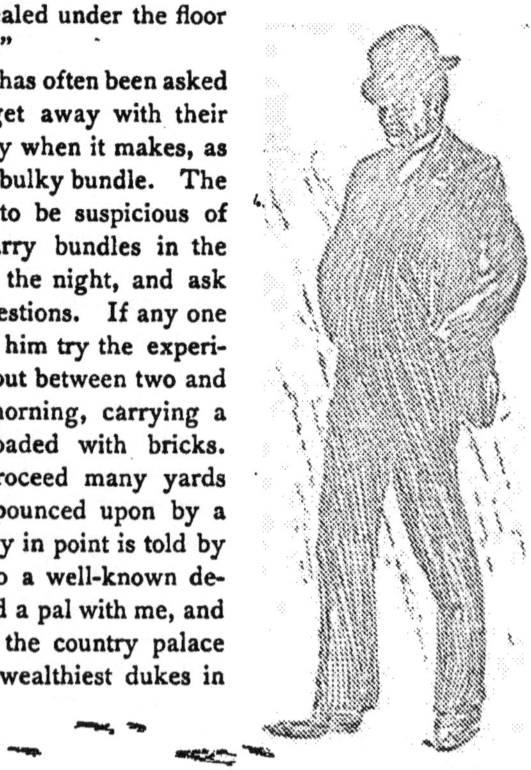

THE BURGLAR WHO WALKED BACKWARD

bags. We had just dragged the sacks into the thicket near the house when the alarm was raised. Think of the tight place we were in, — two o'clock in the morning, and a policeman every thirty yards all around the grounds, every road guarded and every path. Safe enough inside the ring we were, but when daylight came, what would happen? Still the next day dawned, and no trace was found either of the plunder, or of us, and by evening of that same day, it was all melted and sold to the 'fence' in the city. The police were utterly baffled as to how the perpetrators of the robbery got away with two sacks full of plate. No one had passed the cordon of police except a couple of countrymen from the home farm, who were driving a cart to market, containing a slaughtered sheep. Now I might tell the police something that would interest them. If they had turned that sheep over, they would have found, instead of the usual bodily organs, that the carcass contained a valuable collection of silver, and if they had looked under the straw, they might have found the rest of the duke's missing property."

The Second-Story Man. The professional burglar of standing in his profession looks down somewhat with condescension upon the second-story burglar, whose risks are not nearly so great, and whose rewards, of course, are proportionately smaller. The second-story man avoids breaking and entering a house. His fort is obtaining

BURGLARS IN HIDING

an entrance by means of convenient porches, over-hanging boughs of trees, water-conductors, and lightning-rods, up which he climbs with the greatest ease, and enters through an unguarded window in that part of the house where he has planned to make his robbery.

Many successful second-story men work only in the day-time, and are prepared with all sorts of plausible excuses to explain their presence if detected in a house. A burglar engaged in going through the premises after jewels known to be in the house may, in a second's time, assume all the appearance and actions of the honest workman come to repair the plumbing, and by his clever effrontry, escape even after he is detected. Usually, however, the second-story man so plans and times his work as to enter the house when most of the family are absent, and thus avoid the risk of detection.

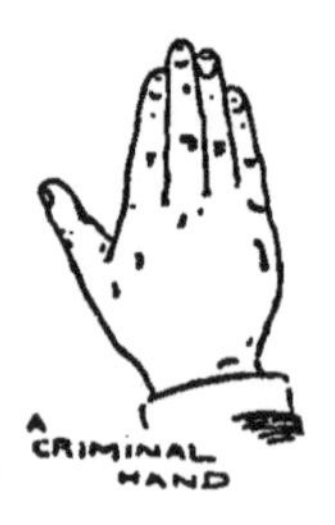

Ordinary Criminal

The ordinary criminal's hand has a peculiarly rough shape, the thumb being very plump and short, while the fingers are uneven and heavy. The small finger is turned inward, and bluntness is the hand's chief characteristic.

SHOT THREE

DIFFICULTIES of BURGLARY

EVERY man who lives by his wits and defies the law of the land must confront difficulties unknown to the ordinary citizen. In the first place, the house must be entered, locks must be forced and picked, burglar-alarms must be circumvented, and every effort made to escape detection. Most people who carry a loaded revolver, or have one in their bed-chamber, think that they are protected. As a matter of fact, a burglar finds the least of his danger at the muzzle of a pistol. In the hands of the excited and frightened citizen who awakes in the middle of the night to find his house being robbed, a revolver is not especially dangerous. Of course, the burglar is likely to get a bullet, but the citizen seems quite as apt to shoot himself or some member of his family as he is a burglar.

Nor do ordinary burglar-alarms present any great difficulty to the expert cracksman. If he knows his business, he has found out beforehand all about these pretty little toys, where they are located, how they are handled, etc. His first care, of course, is to cut the wires or by other means known to him make the burglar-alarm harmless and noiseless. Once silent, he may proceed to pick all the locks in the house, and clad in the darkness and the garment of silence which every burglar knows how to assume, he soon gets away with his ill-gotten plunder.

A pet dog may make an able-bodied burglar more trouble on a midnight expedition than half a dozen pistols or shotguns in the house. These little animals are certainly light sleepers and their bark, while harmless, is very apt to arose every inmate in the place. If the burglar is expert, he has probably cultivated the acquaintance of the dog in advance when he paid court to the kitchen girl at the back door, and a little bottle of chloroform, judiciously placed, puts the dog to sleep very quietly.

The window-bars which are supposed to be such a protection to basement windows also call for remark. They are usually set from four to six inches apart, and are then of very little use, for a miniature screw-jack is made for the profession which will force these bars sufficiently wide apart to allow a thin man to enter.

When going away for the holidays, it is a great mistake to shut up the house. This is simply to make public announcement that the place is unoccupied and may be entered with safety. The wiser plan is to make it look as much occupied as possible and to give notice to the police that you are going away. The next-door neighbors — if you know them to be above suspicion — should also be warned.

OPENING A WINDOW

The question is often asked, where is the safest place to keep one's valuables? My advice is to keep them at your banker's; but if it is really necessary to have them in the house, then the best place is the least likely one.

One communicative burglar gave us two pathetic instances of wasted labor and disappointment that had befallen him. One night he went through a saddler's premises with extraordinary care, but without result, owing to the fact —which subsequently leaked out — that the cash was kept in an old saddle!

The other case was that of a wealthy merchant's house, which was visited in pursuit of cash and securities. None could be found, though the house was thoroughly ransacked. It was afterwards found that they were concealed in a dummy book placed among the volumes in one of the library bookcases.

It is not altogether the wisest plan to keep one's valuables in the bedroom, for the simple reason that a determined burglar, who has learnt their whereabouts, will not hesitate to visit the bedroom, in which case it is very possible that the occupant will not wake up next morning.

I shall conclude this chapter with some account of burglar-proof appliances, as described by Mr. Herbert Howard, a writer in the London magazines, as follows:

Burglars Laugh at Locks. The holiday season is the harvest of the enterprising burglar and the dark days of the late autumn and winter provide a happy hunting-ground for the professional housebreaker.

The need, then, for securely guarding the house against uninvited visitors is one that appeals forcibly to every one who values his own goods and chattels, and is willing to take a little trouble to protect them. The hints given in the present article are the result of a long experience of a very practical character.

If any man knows better than another the relative value of the various modes of protecting a house, it is the professional burglar! He smiles at the futility of many a massive lock and bolt, while, on the other hand, he grinds his teeth with rage as he thinks of certain simple contrivances that have defeated his nefarious designs.

The weakest point about a house is usually a window, and for that reason it is one of the most convenient modes of entry for the burglar. The ordinary window-catch is the most foolish contrivance possible, and must have been invented by somebody who wanted to break in with as little trouble as possible. You have merely to insert a thin putty knife between the sashes and the catch can be pushed back without much difficulty. An attempt is sometimes made to prevent this by the insertion of a screw or other contrivance behind the catch, so that it will not slide back. In this case the judicious use of a jimmy, or crowbar, under the bottom sash will simply force out the screws — always very slight affairs — by which the catch is fastened to the window, and thus the difficulty is overcome without any noise or trouble.

The only really secure mode of fastening a window is by means of strong thumb-screws passing through both sash frames on either side. These screws should work through metal plates let into the sashes. These screws, if properly placed, will resist the application of the crowbar, and, as they are quite inaccessible from the outside of the window, they can only be tampered with by removing the panes of glass.

The door next calls for attention. Usually it is fastened during the day by a light latch, which yields at once to a very mild amount of pressure with a jimmy. For purposes of protection this latch is utterly worthless. The large old-fashioned lock, especially if mortised into the door, is much better. Certainly it can be forced, but only with great difficulty, and it is apt to make a noise like the report of a pistol when it gives way. The best plan, from the burglar's point of view, is to attack the door-post and try to force out the socket into which the bolt of the lock shoots.

Locks used frequently to be picked, and skeleton keys were much in vogue in by-gone days. Now, however, locks have been so greatly improved that they are seldom picked, unless cheap locks are used.

Ordinary door-bolts present no difficulty to the burglar who has his tools with him. They are quickly forced out, screws and all, or they are silently cut through with a saw of diamond steel.

Chains are the best of all fastenings for doors. They are difficult to cut or force, and they are apt to rattle and make

a noise, which is the thing of all others that a burglar dreads most. The presence of the loose chain is not usually discovered until the locks and bolts have been forced, and the first indication of it is generally an audible one. The business of cutting a chain is a troublesome and risky one, owing to the difficulty of keeping it still. There is a special tool for the purpose, but it is not much used.

A glass-panelled door, especially if it has no shutters, is a thing of delight to the intruder, who can only too easily remove the glass and so get access to the locks and bolts. A letter slot without a box is also a helpful contrivance, as it enables him to insert a strong wire loop with which to pull back the latch.

The best way to secure the house door is to provide it with a chain at the extreme top and bottom, in addition to one or two thumb-screws passing through the door into the frame. This will effectually defy the best efforts of the burglar, unless he is prepared to cut out the framework of the door — a long and risky job.

The ordinary window shutters are quite useless, both on account of their weak construction and of the primitive simplicity of the usual fastening, which can be undone without any trouble. Iron shutters are, however, a good protection, but only when fastened by screws in the way we have described.

Inner doors, especially of rooms that contain valuables, should always be locked at night. But the key must be taken away! Many people have the idea that by leaving the key in the lock — of course on the inside of the door — they are making it impossible for the lock to be picked from the outside. As a matter of fact they are simply putting the key into the burglar's hands.

Examine the average door at the hotels and you will find that when the key is in the lock, the end of the barrel slightly projects from the keyhole on the other side of the door. Now the burglar has in his tool-bag a neat little instrument, resembling in shape a very small piano key, with which he is able to grip the projecting end of the barrel, and so turn the key around and unlock the door!

The best of all fastenings for the bedroom or other inner door is a simple wedge of wood pushed under the bottom of the door. If this is correctly shaped and properly placed, it is absolutely impossible to open the door from the outside without cutting a piece out of the panel, and no burglar will risk this with a person sleeping near at hand.

It is, however, sometimes practicable to pass a knife or other article under the door, and so push the wedge back. To prevent this it is only necessary to place some obstacle in the way. A strong screw passed into the floor will serve, especially if it passes through a hole in the wedge.

Burglars have no hesitation in poisoning small dogs when they are in the way of their getting out an especially valuable haul. Sometimes this is done by feeding poison meat through the letter slot, while dogs kept in kennels outside are practically useless for protection, as they may be easily disposed of. If your watch-dog suddenly dies under suspicious circumstances, look out for a burglary within the next few nights.

* * * * * *

Several cases have been known where policemen have taken up the profession of burglary and escaped detection for many years. They yielded to the temptation for gain and fell. I would say, however, on behalf of the police, that cases are known where crooks have gained positions on the police force in order to forward nefarious and nocturnal work of burglary.

Visitor (in jail): Do you never hear the still, small voice of conscience?

Convict: No; I'm hard of hearing.

SHOT FOUR

SOME people imagine that a burglar is forever on the still hunt for plunder; that the breaking into houses forms a nightly part of his program, and that he would be a lonesome individual unless he had a dark lantern in one hand and a jimmy in the other. The truth of the matter is that professional burglars rarely make more than eight or ten good hauls in the course of a season, and that to be out on more than one job inside of a week or ten days would be considered rather dangerous. Of course, there are cases where gangs of burglars are working certain sections of the city where a number of startling robberies are committed one after another, but your careful and successful cracksman limits his work and increases his safety.

The burglar, no doubt, may be a quiet citizen, a householder himself, and one known as a respectable man to his neighbors, and when occasionally he disappears for a week or a fortnight, it is attributed to business in a distant city. His "business" brings him in another rich haul, and when that is disposed of he is on "Easy" street again until inclination or necessity compels him to go forth in quest of other plunder.

Sailors are superstitious, but burglars share that honor with them, for there is no class of individuals who look more carefully to signs of good and evil omen than does your professional "crib cracker." An ex-convict whom I once befriended, in Omaha, and from other sources, I learned the following most common superstitions of thieves and burglars. A black cat is a certain forerunner of disaster to the burglar, and householders who suddenly find their black cats poisoned may take it as a warning that the robbery of their domain has been decided upon, for the criminals take care to destroy their dumb enemies before paying a midnight call. Dogs, on the contrary, they fear but little, however savage they may be, because they take care to carry in their pockets pieces of ivory, a certain cure for dog-bites.

The cries of an infant warn the marauder that misfortune awaits him in the neighborhood. He will not stay in a house if he finds a clock stopped, a broken mirror, or an unframed oil painting; these are infallible omens of disaster.

One of the chief terrors of the burglar is a newly-painted house. Several years ago in a northern town, some disciples of the jimmy broke into a large domicile, but removed nothing, though they favored the next house with a visit the same evening and stole everything of value. They were captured as they were scaling the garden wall, and at the trial one confessed that they had spent eight weeks in making preparations for entering the house from which they removed nothing, and upon doing so found it to have been freshly painted, so transferred their attention to the adjoining building, thereby bringing about their capture.

A criminal studies the weather quite as carefully as the farmer does. He will not perpetrate a crime on the night of a new moon, nor if the orb has a halo or mist round it. And were he to plunder a house during an eclipse, he might as soon give himself up to the law at once, for his days outside of prison walls would be numbered. Even more trifling incidents are of equal significance to the robber. It is bad luck to be followed by a dog, and any undertaking or plundering plan will be abandoned for the time, as it means capture or failure.

If the house selected has crape on the door, to enter would be to court disaster, and to kick against a piece of coal in the road would bring about a similar result.

Pickpockets are very careful not to rob a cross-eyed or club-footed person. To rob a blind man would be to bring down misfortune; but, curiously enough, a blind woman can be victimized with impunity. A stolen purse that contains a battered coin or lock of hair is thrown away intact, or the thief will find himself a prisoner before the day is out.

Talismans are freely carried and implicitly believed in. Burglars in the olden days used to rob a house by the light of a candle made of human fat; but the superstition has nearly died out, owing to the difficulty of procuring material to make them, although it is still prevalent to some extent in Scotland and Ireland. When Burke and Hare were murdering human beings for the medical profession in Scotland, in 1828, it is claimed they also supplied human fat to burglars, the doctors giving Hare a few bottles, as they were told it was a good cure for rheumatism. The medicos treated it as a joke, but Hare sold it to some of the housebreakers he was intimate with. Old nails, broken horseshoes, curiously shaped pebbles, and endless other trinkets have times without number been found in the pockets of captured criminals who have begged that everything else they possessed should be taken from them rather than the talisman to which they pinned their faith. Charles Peace—perhaps the greatest burglar who ever lived—said that his

IT IS BAD LUCK TO BE FOLLOWED BY A DOG

success was due to the pawn-ticket of a violin he pawned when he was a boy, and which he always carried with him.

SAFE-CRACKING

Our chapter on burglary would scarcely be complete without some reference to safe-cracking as a special division of the profession. It is a comparatively small matter to break and enter a house and get away with valuables; but to effect an entrance into a well-guarded bank and succeed in opening safes which have been constructed with every appliance known to the modern safe-builders' art is an entirely different proposition. The "cracking" of such a "crib" is the work of an experienced and especially skilful man.

My friend James Sargent, of Sargent & Greenleaf, Rochester, N. Y., invented the time-lock. Cracksmen would rout the cashier out of his bed with a loaded revolver, and force him to go to the bank and open the safe. But now with the time-lock and other safety electrical safeguards the old burglar tools are worthless; where once tools were used in cutting off locks, tearing off plates, drilling through the lock so as to pick the combination, the cracksman has kept apace of the times and utilizes modern scientific methods to open safes. To open a time-lock they first start in and by hammering the safe break the clock-work. Now they resort to either a large carbon and get their electricity by tapping the trolley-car current and burning circles around the lock, or they make use of a terrible compound invented by Goldschmidt (a man I met in Essen Ruhr, Germany). This compound is named "*thermit*." This is a kind of a mixture of fine aluminum filings or powder and iron oxide.

When this mixture is ignited by suitable means, it gives the extraordinary heat of 3000° C. This compound or concoction, if allowed to flow on top of a safe, will BURN A HOLE clear through most any safe made. I was in Berlin when the first tests were made, and one enterprising safe manufacturer built a safe that was invulnerable to this immense heat, and calls it the "Anti-Thermit" Geldschrank.

CRACKING A SAFE WITH A GRIPPER

Burglary is no longer crude robbing, but an art. The only men who are able successfully to overcome the obstacles of the safemakers and locksmiths, and at the same time avoid the police, are the ones who employ as much care and thought in their work as the successful business man. The man who once turned to burglary as a last resort chose a dark night to force his way into a store, and after hours of work with files and saws forced the door from the safe, can no longer succeed. The only men who succeed in their efforts to open safes now are the ones who often spend weeks studying conditions and preparing their instruments. The resistance offered by the fine grades of steel used in safes usually destroys the tools used to open the locks.

The ingenuity of the safe-cracker is greater only than that of the burglar and sneak thief who depends on the use of skeleton keys and jimmies to make his way past locks and bolts. The skeleton key can only be used in picking simple locks with wards. The burglar's jimmy is often a plain iron bar, sharpened at one end that permits its insertion beneath a window or at the side of a door. Some of the professional burglars, however, carry sectional jimmies that for efficiency are greater than any other burglar tool manufactured.

Safe burglars often purchase old safes and practice on them. Now-a-days they work almost entirely on the lock. The method is first to remove the dial with a special jimmy and then drill a small hole five-eighths of an inch above the spindle, and with a knitting needle or fine wire "pick up" the combination and thus open the safe.

SHOT FIVE

THIEVES and THEIR TRICKS

A THIEF is one who appropriates any kind of property or money to his own use without the consent of the owner. As distinguished from a burglar, a thief does not break into a house or enter in the night time, but takes his plunder wherever he can find it. A thief may gain entrance to a house and steal a valuable diamond, but he uses his sharp wits to pass the door instead of the burglars' jimmy and skeleton keys.

There are thieves of various kinds, from the common sneak thief and shoplifter to the expert pickpocket and clever swindler, who sometimes makes hauls amounting to many thousands of dollars. The use of the word "thief," however, is generally confined to such classes of criminals as shoplifters, pickpockets, and the like. Overcoat thieves ply their trade in the residential sections of the city. They will sometimes ring the front doorbell and ask for the master or mistress of the house, giving some plausible pretext, and usually the name of the party living there. While the servant has gone to tell the mistress of the caller, he quietly picks up what garments are in sight on the hat-rack and makes off with them.

The Venetian blind thief got his name from the practise of the English thieves of making the pretext that they had come to repair the blinds of the house. A thief will call at the door claiming to be a mechanic to look over the house for necessary repairs, and in his rounds will gather up any valuable article that he can lay his hands on. This class of rascal even impersonates the plumber or the gas inspector with equally successful results.

Thieves at church are a very common occurrence. A case is related in London not long ago where a chapel had been furnished with one hundred new Bibles. They were first used at the afternoon service, and when the congregation gathered for evening they had all disappeared. A very common experience of church officers is to find that books disappear gradually; not only books, but hassocks and cushions are taken from houses of worship. Petty robberies from the collection box are not infrequent. In some localities the custom of covering one's offering with one's hand so that other worshipers shall not see the amount given gives the thief his opportunity, for in the rapid passing of the plate it is easy for the skilful professional thief to put in a penny and at the same moment take out a dollar. This is sometimes done by a sticky substance put upon a single finger. Umbrella thieves and pickpockets also ply their trade in church as well as in other places of public gathering.

How can you detect a church thief? is a question I have often asked detectives. There seems to be no real answer; but, as a general rule, it is just as well to look out for your property as carefully when you are in church as when you are out.

Thieves as Wedding Guests. There is scarcely a fashionable wedding where the contracting parties are wealthy that does not suffer from the presence of wedding thieves. For this reason, the more expensive items of jewelry are often imitated in paste before they are put on exhibition among the gifts, while the originals are sent to the bank. The wedding-gift lifter works his game as follows: Disguised as a tradesman or assistant, he gains the confidence of the servants, gets a description of a diamond tiara, or other article of great value, which he then has a duplicate made of set with imitation paste diamonds. He will even go as far as to pay $15 or $100 for a good imitation article. Armed with this and perfectly dressed, he makes his way among the party of

THE VAN THIEF AT WORK

guests and finds it no great risk to adroitly change the counterfeit for the genuine jewel.

Trick of the Van Thief. Vans that are covered entirely with tarpaulin or canvas and have a loose back present opportunities to the van thief. A favorite trick is for the thief to wheel a hand cart, covered with sacking, under which a confederate lies concealed, behind one of these vans. The confederate quickly puts the upper part of his body inside the van, his feet remaining in the cart. Being concealed from view by the loose tarpaulin, he seizes a package, dropping back with it into the cart, which is pushed off at once. A wet day is preferred for this trick, as then not so many people are about, and the driver is likely to be holding his head down as a protection from the rain, in consequence of which he will not look behind.

THE TRICK SATCHEL

The Trick Satchel Thieves. It is when the dark days come round that the railway-station thief most safely conducts his operations. The summer tourist he loves not, for his luggage contains few valuables, and there is then too much light about. A dull afternoon and well-to-do people going off by train are what the platform prowler asks for. And here is shown as a warning, if needs be, an artful appliance that station thieves have used of late years. It looks like an ordinary portmanteau; and so it is with a difference.

It is a specially-made portmanteau, the bottom of which closes up on pressure being applied. Thus, when, as shown in the illustration, the "trick" portmanteau is placed over a smaller one that lies upon the platform, the larger one comes down as a cover over it. By a movement of the thumb of the hand that holds the portmanteau handle, powerful springs are released which tightly grasp the portmanteau that is inside, and it can thus be carried away completely enveloped from sight.

If, therefore, you see a suspicious-looking character hanging about, don't set him down as a genuine passenger just because he has a bag.

Diamond in a Chew of Gum.

One of the cleverest and most unscrupulous diamond thieves I ever heard of perfected a scheme for daylight robbery of unmounted gems which for a time simply defied detectives of London and Paris. The game was played as follows:

A lady, well dressed and looking like a respectable and wealthy matron who might be the wife of a banker or large merchant, enters a jewelry store and asks to see some unmounted diamonds. The clerk shows her the stones, and while she is looking at them, a second lady equally respectable in appearance enters and approaches the same counter. She seems to be interested in diamonds. Suddenly one of the most

THE CHEWING GUM TRICK

valuable gems is missing. The proprietor is summoned, the detectives rush in, and an officer is called. The women, who both declare their innocence, are carefully searched, but the diamond has absolutely disappeared. Eventually both the women are released, but the diamond is never recovered.

The way the trick was played is this:

One of the women (both of whom are members of the gang) deftly concealed the diamond in a piece of chewing gum and sticks it on the under side of the front edge of the counter.

There it remains safely hidden away while the frantic search is going on. A third member of the gang slips in afterward with the crowd of curious and removes the gum containing the diamond and makes off with it.

Said the fond mother: "Never would I call a boy of mine 'Alias' if I had a hundred to name. Men by that name is allus cuttin' up capers. Here's Alias Thompson, Alias Williams, Alias the Night Hawk — all been took up for stealing."

TEACHER: How many of my scholars can remember the longest sentence they ever read?

BILLY: Please, mum, I can.

TEACHER: What? Is there only one? Well, William, you may tell the rest of the scholars the longest sentence you ever read.

BILLY: Imprisonment for life.

SHOT SIX

The ARISTOCRAT of THIEVERY

THERE are kings of crime as well as kings of finance. Much the same talent which enables John D. Rockefeller to pile up a thousand million dollars or Henry H. Rogers to control unnumbered millions in Wall Street, applied in a different direction, develops that high grade of criminal whose robberies are exploited in scare-head stories in newspapers, and are the talk of the country for many days. The case which occurred at Liverpool a short time ago was the work of a bright man. The circumstances related to me by a newspaper man are as follows: "One day Messrs. Oldfield & Co., of Liverpool, received a telegram purporting to come from Mrs. Brattlebank, of Garston, then staying in London, ordering a quantity of diamonds to be sent to her Garston residence. Mrs. Brattlebank being a wealthy customer and well known to this jewelry house, a package of valuable stones was made up and sent by registered post, after being insured for $5,000.

After the arrival of the package in Garston, a well-dressed gentleman representing himself to be Mr. Laing Miller, a wealthy South African ship owner and a friend of the Brattlebanks, called at the residence, having previously explained by telephone that he was coming to take the package to Mrs. Brattlebank in London. The whole affair seemed so open and aboveboard, and the appearance of Mr. Miller so honest and convincing, that the valuable package was handed over to him without question. Neither Mr.

Miller, who is now suspected to be one of the most expert confidence men in the Kingdom, nor the diamonds have ever been seen since."

The Swindler Who Lowered a Check. The crime of raising a check is often attempted, and sometimes successfully, but it is seldom that a criminal attempts to lower the figures on a check and cash it for a less sum than it was made out for. The following incident occurred in Wall Street not long ago, showing that the man who conceived it must have had a ready wit and a clever brain, as well as considerable daring to put it into execution. It is said that this ingenious swindler had already realized between two and three thousand dollars by his startling new method of lowering checks.

For instance, a stock exchange broker sells one thousand shares of a stock to ten customers in blocks of one hundred shares at 91. Each purchaser prepares a check for $9,100 for the seller when the messenger boys make their rounds. If the checks are not ready when the messenger calls out to the cashier, who usually cannot see the boy, he is told to come back later.

This swindler follows a messenger boy, and when the boy is told to return later the fellow returns himself in a short time and gets the check, which is readily handed over to him.

Having secured the check for $9,100 the swindler hurries away, and, knowing that safety does not lie in presenting the check for so large an amount, reduces it to $910, makes it payable to bearer by the use of chemicals, and secures the money.

A Daring Train Robbery. Among the clever coups that have come to my attention here is one related by an ex-convict, and published recently in an English periodical which presents some rather interesting features. The writer says: "A certain lady of high social position was known to possess an exceptionally valuable collection of jewelry, and some of us had long been casting covetous eyes upon it. One day she started from St. Pancras in the Scotch express for he husband's seat in the Highlands, the jewelry being securely packed in one of her numerous trunks. These were duly placed in the luggage van, which was locked, and only opened by the guard at the two or three places where the express stopped. No one save the railway servants entered the van or left it, neither had the doors been opened while the train was in motion. But when the trunk in question was unlocked far away in Scotland, the jewel case was gone, and from that day to this not the slightest clue has been found as to its disappearance. Here was a case for a Sherlock Holmes or a Martin Hewitt, but either these gentlemen were not forthcoming, or they totally failed to solve what is, perhaps, the most mysterious railway robbery of recent days.

"Let me lift the veil and show how the little job was worked. Two men, both of whom are still making a very comfortable income as railway thieves, got to know of the lady's proposed journey, and discovered the train by which she intended to travel. Accordingly, they also traveled north by that train, though they did not go as far as Scotland. On the contrary, they only booked to Leeds. Their luggage consisted of two portmanteaus and a massive wooden trunk, strongly hooped and padlocked. It was an honest, straightforward-looking trunk, but any one who examined it very

THE TRUNK "TRICK ROBBERY"

closely might have discovered a quantity of small holes in its sides, practically concealed by the iron hoops, between which and the woodwork there was at intervals a slight space. That trunk did not contain the large assortment of wearing apparel that might have been supposed; in fact, it only contained one suit of clothes, and that suit encased the limbs of a boy of fourteen!

"As soon as the train was well on its journey, one end of the trunk opened, and the small boy emerged. With the aid of a goodly stock of skeleton keys and pick-locks — the English hamper locks can be opened with a button-hook, they are so simple — he opened the various hampers bearing her ladyship's name, and presently discovered the jewel case, which he removed to his own box. He then locked up the trunks, returned to his hiding-place, closed the sliding panel, curled himself up comfortably in the box, and went to sleep for the rest of the journey.

"At Leeds the two men alighted, called a porter, who got their luggage out of the van for them, and then drove in a cab to a certain temperance hotel in Briggate, where, in the privacy of the room they had secured, the boy was let out of the box, and the jewel case gleefully examined. Its contents traveled back to London by the next train, and were safely on the continent before the news of the robbery had reached Scotland Yard."

A Check for $30,000. A single "plant" on a Chicago bank was pulled off recently, whereby the clever swindler coppered out $30,000 for himself with very little effort. The bank officers tried to hush the matter up as much as possible, and for the sake of the depositors I shall not give the name of the institution, but the facts which I am certain are substantially as follows: A depositor of several years' standing appeared a few days ago in the bank president's office with a draft on London for £6,000, which was perfectly good. The depositor informed the president he desired to deposit this London draft, and at the same time to check against it, presenting his check for $30,000 for the president to O. K.

The latter put his initials on it and thought no more of the transaction. The depositor then went out into the bank and deposited his London draft, and on the following day presented a check for $30,000, which was paid, the teller knowing that that amount was to his credit on the books. Later in the day he again appeared at the window and presented the check for $30,000, which had been initialed by the president. This check was also paid. Nothing more has since been seen of the depositor.

EMBEZZLER'S WIFE: You are a thief and a criminal. Never speak to me again!

EMBEZZLER: But I stole it all for your sake.

EMBEZZLER'S WIFE: Yes, but didn't you go and give it all back again? — *Cincinnati Commercial-Tribune.*

"What did that man do to make himself so famous?" asked the inquirer, gazing curiously at an individual who formed the center of a social group.

"To the best of my knowledge," replied the cynic, "he did the public."

SHOT SEVEN

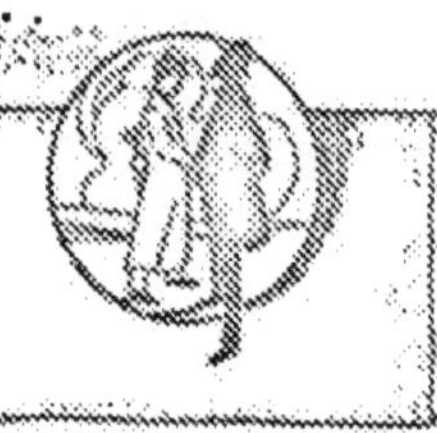

PICKPOCKETS at WORK

AMONG the most interesting classes of thieves is the pickpocket, whose clever subterfuges and skill of hand have been so often exploited in novel and story-book. Your professional pickpocket is naturally a rover, and travels the country over, attending large gatherings. Of professional pickpockets there are a number of types, each adapted to the class of "work" in which he engages.

It is the usual opinion that a pickpocket is a forbidding and suspicious looking fellow, but a glance at the rogues' gallery in any police headquarters will show you that they look much like ordinary individuals, and are of more than average intelligence. The pickpocket is usually very well dressed and of prepossessing appearance. Those who seek to make only large hauls are entertaining talkers and easy in their manner. They are generally self-possessed and, while dexterous, are very cautious in their operations.

It is needless to say that women make the most patient as well as the most dangerous pickpockets. It is simply amazing how quickly an expert pickpocket, with a delicate touch, seemingly accidental, will locate the resting-place of a well-filled purse or other article of value which he chooses to abstract. When once discovered they follow their intended victims until the proper opportunity comes. A common pickpocket trick is for the operator to carry a shawl or overcoat carelessly over the left arm, and to take a seat on the right side of the person they intend to rob in a street-car or other vehicle.

THE FEMALE PICKPOCKET

Sometimes a small and very sharp knife is used to cut the side of the dress or pantaloons of the victim, so that the purse may be abstracted without going into the pocket directly. Others of this light-fingered gentry wear light overcoats with large pockets removed. They will endeavor to stand near a person, preferably a woman, who is paying her fare and has displayed a well-filled purse. The pickpocket then carelessly throws his coat over her dress, and by inserting his hand through the outside opening of his own pocket, quietly proceeds to abstract her purse. Pickpockets either work alone or in pairs, or what is called a mob. Most female pickpockets seem to prefer to work alone, sometimes, however, working in conjunction with a man thief to whom they pass their plunder, and thus make detection impossible if they are suspected and searched.

The mob is a gang of expert pickpockets under the direction of a leader who has had experience, and knows all the tricks. Their usual game is to frequent some crowded platform or a railway station, and raise an apparent row in which two men seem to engage in a scuffle or quarrel and come to blows. Others rush in attempting to separate them, and the attention of the whole crowd of people is for the moment directed strongly that way. At the same moment other single light-fingered members of the same gang crowd in with the citizens who are being jostled, and abstract their pocketbooks and watches without any trouble. Recently a gang has successfully worked in several of the subway stations in Boston, and the same gang has successfully plyed this vocation in New York, Chicago, and Philadelphia.

The false-arm game, or the "third mit," as it is known

to the professional pickpocket, is said to be little employed in this country now. A loose cape overcoat is worn in one of the sleeves of which a false arm and hand are fixed. Thus a detective who may be watching the pickpocket will see apparently both of his hands in view, while in reality the light skilful fingers of the operator's left hand are going through the pockets of the man beside of whom he is standing. This dodge is very much employed on the continent by shoplifters.

One of the many fertile dodges by which a pickpocket escapes detection is known as the horse-dodge. The thief so arranges as to meet his victim by the side of a horse standing by the curbstone. He has previously located the watch or purse he wishes to lift, and with a quick blow he knocks his victim's hat over his eyes, grabs the pocketbook or watch or whatever else he is after, and immediately darts under the horse, and hides himself in the traffic on the other side. By the time the victim has got the use of his eyes, and is able to look around, the thief has entirely disappeared, and he would not be apt to look in the right direction, at any rate.

In the outskirts of London, among the small shops, a rather unusual trick has been played frequently upon unsuspecting shopkeepers. Two men in earnest argument over some matter enter a small grocery store and approach the proprietor who is behind his till. One man says to the proprietor, "My friend and I have gottten into an argument over a peculiar matter which we believe you can settle for us. I have bet him that my hat," taking off an old-fashioned stove-pipe hat, "will hold more than four quarts of molasses, while he contends that it will hold hardly three quarts. We are willing to buy the molasses if you will fill this hat and prove the question to decide the bet." The shopkeeper good-humoredly agrees, and brings the hat brimful with sticky molasses, at which one of the thieves slaps it over the shopkeeper's head, and before he can extricate himself and call help they have robbed the till and disappeared.

SHOT EIGHT

BEGGARS and DEAD BEATS

THERE probably is not a reader of this book who has not frequently been accosted on the street corners by the poorly-dressed, shivering wretch who asks in a whining voice for a coin or two to get him a night's lodging.

Who has not experienced the mingled feeling of repugnance and pity which their stories are intended to produce? Who has not, rather than run the chance of turning away an honest man in real distress, put his hand in his pocket and dropped a dime or a quarter into grimy, outstretched fingers and went on his way more than half convinced that he had paid money to a fraud.

CHIEF OF A BEGGAR GANG

Beggars there have been since civilization created the distinctions of wealth and poverty and must needs be till a higher, better civilization makes misery and crime impossible or unnecessary. For ages the mendicant has flourished, plying his vocation on the credulous and making profit out of the fact that humanity and religion make almsgiving a virtue. In the Middle Ages beggars became so numerous that they threatened to overrun the continent. The begging "friars" and other religious orders encouraged it and the beggars throve. To-day the modern law in most lands forbids begging, but still most people would be surprised to know to what extent it is practised,—that is, to what lengths and in what numbers the fraudulent cheating professional beggar preys upon the alms-giving, over-credulous public.

I have watched the beggars of most of the great cities of America and Europe, and have made some little investigation into their methods, and I do not hesitate to say that in ninety cases out of a hundred the man who asks for alms on the street corner is a cheat and a fraud. If the public would take my advice and absolutely refrain from giving to beggars, this nuisance might soon be done away with. If the beggar no longer found his calling profitable, he would soon go to work or seek other fields of activity.

As a rule, the beggars we see upon our streets belong to well-organized gangs and their individual members are controlled by a chief whose word is law. For simple begging the territory is laid out and each man keeps within his own beat. At night they assemble at some cheap lodging-house, where each one turns over his day's "takings" to the leader, who acts as treasurer and even often deposits a fund in the bank to be used in emergencies or for bail money. A certain portion of the income for the day is divided each night among all members, either equally or in certain shares agreed upon. It is said that a leader or treasurer is always faithful to his trust, for if he were to appropriate the money, he would at once be barred out of the "United Order of American Beggars" or "Sons of Rest," and blacklisted all over the country.

"KID" JOHNSON

Sometimes the leaders will take in young boys and train them in the art of deceiving the public. Chief Watts tells one such story of a young man known as "Kid" Johnson, an orphan boy who came under the influence of "Frisco's Slim," the burly leader of a gang of Boston beggars. This wiley mendicant filled the lad's mind with stories about easy money and showed him how he (Frisco Slim) had "doctored" his arm with a chemical to give it the appearance of a frightful burn.

"With that arm," said Frisco, "I collar many a dollar every day of my life. I'll fix your arm in another style that'll catch on great!"

So the mere boy was enrolled as "Kid Johnson" and taken to a resort known to the gang, where his arm was put in a plaster cast, and he was sent out to beg on the street. His scanty clothing was thin and ragged, his toes peeped through his shoes, and he looked the picture of weariness and hunger. In a short time the "Kid" proved one of the best money-getters of the whole gang. But his masters' demands grew faster than his ability to bring in the coin. He was required to bring in a certain amount each day and ill-treated if it fell short. His life was that of a slave. He was finally rescued by the police and given a chance to reform and lead an honest life, but the taint of crime had entered his nature and he soon ran away to take to the road and street again.

The Magic Cap. A German organist who came to St. Petersburg from Orenburg on a visit to his relatives met with an adventure which caused him to wonder whether he had by accident been transported into the Mystic East and carried back to the times of the Arabian Nights. The story of his adventure might well be entitled "The Magic Cap," and it will be seen that it bears a strong resemblance to the story of "Aladdin and his Wonderful Lamp."

On arriving at St. Petersburg the German visitor purchased a cap, which he thought would be more comfortable than his ordinary headgear for exploring the town, with which he was not well acquainted. On arriving home in the evening after his first day's sightseeing he was greatly surprised to find in the pockets of his overcoat two purses, one of them containing over ten pounds.

He marvelled greatly at his mysterious luck, and sallied out again next day. When he came home again he found in his pockets several more purses, and began to feel alarmed. When on the third day he came home with another windfall in his pockets he became frightened. But his Teutonic commonsense would not allow him to believe in the existence of magic, and he decided to have recourse to the prosaic police force in order to elucidate the mystery.

Accordingly, he sought out the chief of police, and told him all the facts. The astute official examined him closely as to the clothes he was wearing, and particularly as to the cap he had bought in St. Petersburg, and on receiving his replies sent the German with a policeman to the hatter's shop. The shopkeeper explained that the cap was of an exceptional kind. Some time ago a man had called on him and given him a large piece of English cloth, out of which he was to make fifteen caps of exact similarity. On concluding this order the hatter found that he had a piece of the cloth left over, and of this he made an extra cap, the identical one which was sold to the German.

On the strength of this information the chief of police arranged for a detective to accompany the German on his next day's sightseeing, and then the mystery of the "magic cap" was fully cleared up. Watching his charge carefully, the detective saw various men lounge furtively up to the German and transfer something from their hands to his pockets. On each occasion the man thus discovered was arrested, and in the course of two or three days, during which the same plan was pursued, the police made prisoners of about a dozen men. They turned out to be a gang of pickpockets and all wore a cap of the same pattern as that purchased by the German. Their plan was to pass on their plunder to a confederate, for whom the German had been mistaken.

A very favorite trick of begging-letter writers is to try to obtain money on behalf of some bogus society in which they think the celebrity written to might be interested. The swindler will even go so far as to get the name of a fictitious institution printed on a number of letters, and writing as the secretary ask for a subscription. Probably in nine cases out of ten this will be sent without any further inquiries being made by the recipient of the request, the printed letter-paper being considered a sufficient guarantee as to the genuineness of the appeal.

Often professional beggars are actually men of wealth. Not long ago a beggar died in New York who had eleven bank-books concealed about his person, with deposits amounting to thousands of dollars. Beggars frequently own real estate, stocks, and bonds. This is putting a beggar on horseback with a vengeance.

An actual incident of this kind was disclosed in one of our largest cities not long ago. In a smart little villa in one of the suburbs lived an equally smart young married couple. Mr. Cecil Brown Smith was the name on the door-plate, and every morning Mr. Smith went into the city, and every evening came home. If a neighbor asked about business, he would reply,

"Oh, pretty good, I can't complain."

So the pretty little wife was happy from morning till night and all went well.

In the city, shuffling painfully along one of the principal streets, a miserable object had for some time touched the hearts (and pockets) of stockbrokers and city men. Even the poor, almost beggars themselves, have dropped their mite into the cigar-box full of matches which he carried in his one hand, for he was an object of such abject misery.

One arm hung helpless by his side, his head hung with the weakness of paralysis. His right leg was paralyzed, and he laboriously dragged it after him.

No one on earth would have supposed a connection between the crippled match-seller, always so grateful for alms, and the snug suburban home. But for some reason two disguised detectives for some hours took a close interest in the beggar's business.

When the match-vender's "day's work" was over, one of the detectives followed him and witnessed an astonishing transformation.

First, said the detective, the lame man dragged himself to an adjacent tobacconist's shop, where he changed his silver and coppers into bills. Here, too, he left the cigar-box and the matches until the morrow, and then he boarded a car to a cheap lodging-house, and by the time he had arrived there his lameness had disappeared and he went up the steps two at a time.

Finally, he went home to the smart little villa already described. He was the gentleman who lived there with his wife and child.

One afternoon, as the match-peddler was shuffling painfully along with the cigar-box as before, Detective Number One suddenly confronted him:

"You're an impostor," said the detective.

"Can you prove it?" demanded the beggar.

The officer said he could, and at once arrested him for begging. As the prisoner declared he could not walk, and objected to the publicity of an ambulance, he was conveyed to the police station in a cab.

In the dock at the police station, he presented the appearance of an intelligent and fairly well-dressed man of twenty-nine.

One of the most amazing features of the case was a statement that Smith's wife was surprised to hear of her husband's "goings on." She knew nothing about Smith's occupation in the city.

Begging cards covered with the worst kind of doggerel "poetry" are often used by beggars. Who has not at one time or another received one like the following entitled "The Cripple's Appeal"?

Kind people, do not fear me,
  Or turn me from your door.
I ask you but to hear me,
  Or read my story o'er.
'Tis the same old tale of hardship,
  Misfortune, and of woe,
That others have told before me,
  And you've heard it all, I know.
From house to house in the city
  This little appeal I've made,
And it's with a hope for pity
  That I ask you for your aid.

Did you ever give a nickel or a dime to the person who handed you such a card? If you did, you gave to an out-and-out professional beggar. Indeed, nine times out of ten—yes, ninety-nine times out of one hundred—every coin that goes into the tin cup or the hand of a street beggar goes to a fraud of the worst description.

VISITOR (at the gaol): Poor, poor man! May I offer you this bunch of flowers?

MAN BEHIND THE BARS: You've made a mistake, miss. The feller that killed his wife and children is in the next cell. I'm yere for stealing a cow.

"It would be helpful to you," said the prison visitor, "if you could take some motto and try and live up to it."

"That's right," replied the convict; "I'd like to select, for instance, 'We are here to-day and gone to-morrow.'"

SHOT NINE

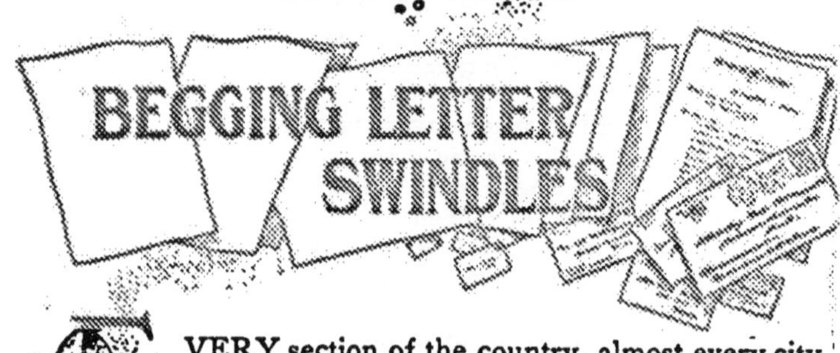

EVERY section of the country, almost every city, has one or more begging letter writers, who ply their trade with greater or less success, and exercise their arts upon the simple and credulous.

These clever rascals range all the way from the ignorant crook that writes a pitiful story of want and misery, and who neither receives nor expects more than a few dollars at a time, to the master of the craft, who goes about it like a regular business, has a well-organized office and a force of stenographers and clerks, who are kept busy day in and day out sending off and receiving mail.

Several remarkable cases have been unearthed only lately, where the fake was receiving hundreds of letters daily, the large majority of them containing money. The post-office authorities, however, have been getting after this class of rogues very sharply of late, and any organized plundering by the use of the mails, is almost certain to come to an untimely end sooner or later.

If any one has reason to believe that a business of the kind is conducted on fraudulent lines, a complaint to one of the post-office inspectors in any large city will quickly bring a "fraud order" against the party, restraining them from use of the mails, and a rigid investigation follows. Then the game is up, and it's back to the "tall timber" for them. It is a well-known fact, however, that this recourse to the "fraud order" is frequently used by unprincipled persons, out of spite and to obtain revenge upon those who are actually conducting a legitimate business. The fraudulent advertisement is often an adjunct to the bogus letter scheme, and designed to get names to whom a special kind of letter may be written. One of the most daring schemes of this kind was unearthed a short time ago in New York City. A man fitted up a suite of offices in elegant style in one of the large office buildings. He then traveled to South Dakota, and under the laws of that State, incorporated a stock company, with a capitalization of five million dollars. It was called a commercial and mining company. Returning to New York, he instructed the Press Clipping Bureau to save him the obituary notices of all males that died in the States other than New York — just far enough away from the center of operations to be comfortable for him.

Using these obituary notices for guides, he would write to the dead man, notifying him that the last payment was due on the five hundred or one thousand shares of stock which he had bought at fifty cents a share. He congratulated the man on his foresight on investing in this stock, as it had gone up several points, and was still rising in value. He begged that a remittance in final payment of this stock should be sent at once.

A beautifully engrossed certificate of stock was enclosed in the letter to the dead man, and the inevitable result was that the surviving relatives, thinking the departed one had bought this stock quietly and forgotten to mention it, sent on a check for all the way from five hundred to one hundred dollars as requested. It was one of the prettiest schemes that has been worked for a long time, and the actual amount of money realized by the swindler will never be known. Such a "snap" could not last long, however, and the promulgator of the swindle was soon detected and brought to trial.

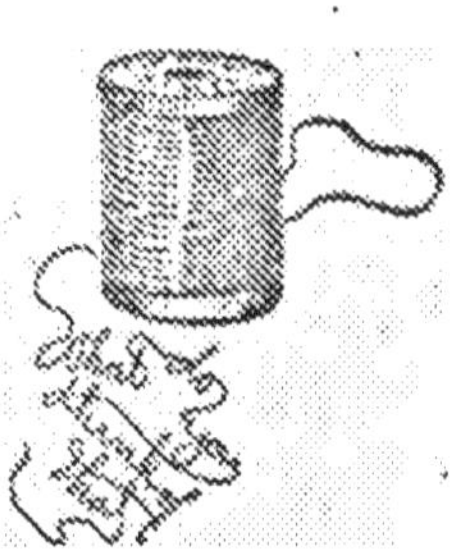

One man advertised to sell ten yards of good silk for twenty-five cents, and so worded his announcement as to suggest a bankrupt sale or smuggled goods. For a time he reaped a rich harvest. Money came thick and fast. To each of his dupes he mailed ten yards of sewing silk!

Another rascal offered a complete and perfect sewing-machine for one dollar. He, also, gathered in the dollars at a rapid rate, till Uncle Sam put a stop to his operations — he sent his victims a common sewing needle!

This is quite in line with the fellow who advertised a few years ago to tell a sure way of getting rid of chinch bugs for one dollar. After the victim had sent the dollar, he received by mail a card upon which was printed the following: —

> **Catch the chinch bug. Hold it by the legs carefully between the thumb and forefinger. Lay its head on the anvil, and hit it with a hammer as hard as you can.**

Many of these advertisements are inserted merely to receive names and addresses of credulous people. The lists of names are then sold or rented out to fake mail-order houses, who proceed to circularize them.

Chain letter schemes are now declared illegal, but for some time a number of clever dodges of this kind were worked throughout the United States as well as on the continent. A brief description of one of these schemes will show the character of this kind of enterprise: —

The scheme was where a trip to the Paris Exposition, with two hundred dollars for expenses, was offered as a prize. Each person entering the contest was required to pay thirty cents, then send to friends two letters, requesting them to send their names to the original promoter, and send duplicate letters to two of their friends, the operation to be repeated indefinitely.

Each person writing to the original promoter was to receive an offer, allowing him to start a chain on his own account, on payment of thirty cents, the trip and money going to the one whose chain brings out the largest number of letters. The ostensible object was to secure names for employment at the exposition.

SHOT TEN

TRICKS of BUNCO MEN

SOMETHING for nothing has ever tempted the simple and unsophisticated; indeed, it is a trait of human nature upon which the swindler everywhere, and in all ages, has relied to his profit.

The origin of the term "bunco" comes from an old English game of chance in which a checkered cloth covered with numbers and stars is covered with a hood called a "bunco." The game was to throw dice which counted up to a certain concealed number. The man who knew the game was called the "bunco man," or the banker, and later when this form of swindle became notorious the term was corrupted into "bunco." To-day the word is used to denote almost any swindle where the victim is made to believe he is to receive a large sum of money or valuables, and then gets nothing at all.

The real Simon Pure Bunco Game, as practised in the United States some years ago by Tom O'Brien, the King of Bunco Men, was played as follows: The victim, some wealthy farmer usually, was lured to a room at a hotel and a game was proposed. A confederate took the part of another player. A pack of forty-eight cards in eight sets, each set numbered from one to six was produced, shuffled, and dealt out eight cards to each player. The total sum of the numbers in each hand was then compared with the number carrying a prize on the chart. If it corresponded, the hand won the prize.

THE BUNCO MEN AND THE VICTIM

The cards are gravely counted and compared. The dealer then says to the confederate and dupe:

"Gentlemen, you have drawn the grand conditional advertising prize. You're entitled to $10,000 apiece on condition that you prove yourselves worth $50,000, and promise to advertise our battery, whether you win or lose. You will have to put up $10,000 apiece against the $10,000 prize; then you draw once more. If you draw a star number you get only the $10,000 prize and your money back. If you draw any other number you get its prize added to your own money and the big prize."

The confederate says he is worth more than $50,000 and declares his intention of going and getting the $10,000 stake. The dupe is also persuaded to put up the cash and both winners go away to get the money. They return and the money is put up. Four cards are dealt each. The total of each hand is twenty-eight.

"Why, gentlemen," says the bunco man in apparent surprise, "twenty-eight is the 'State number,' the total blank! You have lost all!"

The confederate pretends to be very much broken up, condones with his "fellow victim" and gets him out of the room as soon as he can. In a few moments he gives the farmer the slip, joins his partner, and they escape from town as quickly as possible.

Such is the principle of the bunco game, and it is worked under many guises with cards, dice, at the pool or billiard table — our pool-room bunco is known as "*selling the lemon*," as bets are made on the yellow ball — but always with the idea of making the victim believe he is going to get something for nothing.

A variation of the bunco game, often played in the farming districts, is for a well-dressed, plausible man to drive up to a well-to-do farmer's home and inquire if he knows of a good farm for sale. If he does, he is invited to drive with the stranger to take a look at it and give his advice. The farmer finds his new acquaintance bright and entertaining. The property is reached and the sharper with apparent satisfaction inspects the land and buildings, and closes a bargain without much haggling. In the course of conversation the man from the city flashes a big roll of bank notes of high denomination and the farmer is duly impressed.

As they drive homeward a confederate will appear who stops the carriage to make some inquiry. The three enter into conversation and good-natured chaffing leads up to a proposal of some game of cards or bet. The farmer is induced to take a hand, the first swindler offering to put up his half of the stake. When the two "partners" — the farmer and the first swindler — have won a large sum the loser asks for proof of their ability to make good their stake. The first swindler produces the cash, and the farmer drives with him to the next town to draw his money out of the bank to make good his claim.

Now comes the rapid denouncement. The first swindler asks the farmer to oblige him by taking charge of all the money, including the money with which he is to buy the farm, until he can return and close the bargain. The countryman, naturally pleased at this confidence, is induced to put his own money in the same convenient tin box which the stranger has ready. At that point the stranger and the farmer part. The former to parts unknown, the latter with his precious tin box under his arm, and when he gets home

he finds, instead of money, that the box is filled only with heavy folded papers to give it the same weight. A rapid shift has been made before his eyes without his detecting it; his money is gone, and two adroit scoundrels are far away.

Among the most famous (or infamous) bunco men of this country are Tom O'Brien, mentioned above, William Raymond, "Doc" Mincheon, George Post, William Barrocks, Lewis Ludlow, and Clay Wilson. O'Brien is serving a life sentence for murder, but Post is supposed to be still at his old tricks.

Jacob Sindheim, alias "Al" Wise, has a star game. His lay is to persuade a gullible person that he has a secret process by means of which genuine gold coins can be "sweated" or robbed of a portion of their gold, by a certain solution, without impairing their appearance. Several times he has induced speculative individuals without conscience, to construct tanks in the basement of their houses and put in from $10,000 to $20,000 in gold pieces for treatment. Twenty days are to be required for the process. Before that time he removes all the gold, which is needless to say has lost not a grain of its weight, and makes his escape. The victim, after getting tired of waiting, opens the tank to find a liberal deposit of paving-stones instead of gold coins. Then he wakes up.

If men did not try and get something for nothing they might often be able to retain that which they have.

One of the latest dodges of a bunco nature is a bogus express company which caters to those who never receive packages by express, but who want to. In a large room above its showy office a force of skilled workmen are employed, manufacturing bundles and filling them with old bricks and newspapers.

The express company, having made up a convincing-looking parcel, sends out a postal card to its prospective victim on which it says:

MR. E. Z. MARK STEINER, 398 JAY STREET:

Please furnish us with your address, as there is a package addressed to you at our office.

COMEANDGO EXPRESS CO.

The fact that the express company has written to him at his address to ask him what his address is does not strike the victim as strange. The "company" does it in order that it may get in writing from Mr. Steiner a request to deliver the package, thus making him its debtor to the extent of the "express charges," usually $2.

"When I was once in danger from a tiger," said an old convict, "I tried sitting down and staring at him, as I had no weapons."

"How did it work?" asked his cell mate.

"Perfectly — the tiger didn't even offer to touch me."

"Strange. How do you account for it?"

"Well, sometimes I've thought it was because I sat down on a top branch of a very tall tree."

ARRESTED WHEN DEAD.

A splendid funeral procession was proceeding from Hongo, Japan, to bury the remains of Tarofi, the head of a gambling den, when the police stopped the ceremony as the deceased was believed to be an escaped convict. The accusation was found to be true, and the dead man was taken to the prison burial-ground.

SHOT ELEVEN

The GAME of WITS

WHEN the corn-husking is over and the county fairs begin their annual three and four-day sessions in a thousand agricultural centers, a silent army of confidence men and swindlers make ready for their richest harvest of the year! The county fairs are rich fields for their particular work, and they intend to make the most of their opportunities.

The three-shell-game man has been a feature of such gatherings from time immemorial. The game in some form or other has been played ever since Rome was founded. Three half walnut shells or metal covers are used and a small and exceedingly lively pea made of soft rubber. The gaping yokel is invited to pick the shell under which the "pea" reposes. The clever manipulator tosses it from one to another, then, with an apparent awkward twist, seems to throw it under a certain one. The rustic backs his opinion with his coin. The shells are lifted. The former was mistaken and pays for his experience.

It is only another case of where the manipulation of the hand deceives the eye. They say that a new "sucker" is born every minute. Certain it is that this old game finds its dupes as plentiful as in the days of our grandfathers. The callow youth of to-day is willing to bet his last cent that he can put his finger on the shell that covers the "pea" for he has seen it put there!

But if the unsuspecting countryman is an easy mark for

cheats at his county fairs, he is often even more "accessible" when he comes to the city. The following story copied entire from the New York *Telegraph* is especially good on account of its breezy style and true-to-life description of the methods of the quick-witted gentry. The story is entitled:

Was Kind to Strangers.

"Oh, the shame of it, that S. G. Dabdoub of Jersey City should journey all the way from his native heath to Boston and there accept bad money from a stranger!

"Hideous circumstance! Malicious fate! If there is a Mrs. Dabdoub, what will she say?

"Dabdoub! The very name smacks of caution.

"But when he reached Boston and saw all the houses, and still was gazing upon them from his point of vantage at the railroad station, a stranger who had been peering furtively from the dense underbrush observed him.

"After retiring behind a freight-car and throwing a few joyous hand-springs, as if pleased at something, the stranger muttered:

"'He will do. I have not waited in vain. To-night in my palatial residence there shall be joy and feasting and seeming laughter. Ah! it is good to live!'

"After this mysterious and ingrowing conversation, sometimes yclept monologue, the stranger dashed up to Mr. Dabdoub, of far Jersey, and said in his panting tone

MR. DABDOUB'S ARRIVAL.

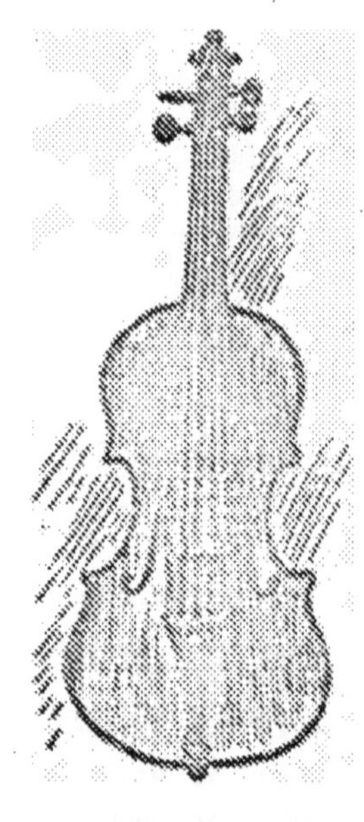

of a man who had gone seven furlongs under the spur of cruel circumstances:

"'Can you give me change for a fifty dollar bill?'

"Mr. Dabdoub could, would, and did, and the stranger, without stopping to count the money, placed a bill in the Jersey man's hands, expressed his thanks in a monosyllable, and hurried away.

"Horrors! The bill he left behind was a Confederate one.

"Mr. Dabdoub, incensed, pursued, but the stranger wore the seven league boots of successful guilt, and it is unlikely that Nick Carter could have caught him.

"Dabdoub went to the police, who wept with him and addressed him as if he had been a public meeting."

Here is another adroit swindle that might almost be considered better than a gold brick.

Some time ago a young fellow with a violin under his arm entered a market-place in one of our large cities, made his purchase, and then found himself short of money. However, he offered the fiddle as security, while he fetched the necessary amount of cash. Scarcely had he left the place when a well-dressed man entered and saw the fiddle on the counter. He examined it and cried out that it was a Stradivarius.

"Why, I'll give you $300 for it," he said.

The shopkeeper refused to sell it without consulting the owner, and the second stranger went away leaving five dollars for the refusal of the treasure. Presently, the first rogue returned, was informed of the offer, and said he would agree, providing the tradesman would give him $150 down. The victim complied, and neither of the swindlers ever returned. The fiddle was worth about $1.50.

But don't get the idea that farmers and small shopkeepers

are the only prey of the bunco man, the swindler and the confidence man. A city man on a farm the first time and trying to run it, is of a greener green than a farmer in a city buying gold bricks. Here are some games successfully played on the dwellers in cities.

The Clever "Sofa Game"

Of all the men who live by their wits, the English crook who conceived and carried into successful execution the so-called "sofa game" certainly deserves the palm. So ingenious, so daring, and yet so simple, is this scheme that it deserves a special description. The reader will notice that it partakes both of the nature of a confidence game and a first-class burglary job.

The game requires the cooperation of several members of a gang, one of whom must be a boy or a young man of small stature and slender physique. Sometimes a young woman is employed, who, if discovered, throws herself upon the mercy of the householder. The gang first selects the residence of some wealthy citizen. If inside information about the silver and jewels to be looted can be secured, so much the better. The habits of the members of the family are closely observed and then at an hour when the fewest possible people are at home the plan is put into execution.

THE "SOFA TRICK."

This is what happens:

A furniture wagon drives up to the house and a well-dressed

man of respectable appearance and plausible address rings the front-door bell. The door is opened, the following conversation ensues:

"Is this the residence of Mr. John Rahner?"

"Yes, but Mr. Rahner is not at home."

"Dear, dear, that is unfortunate! But, however, it does not matter. I have been commissioned as chairman of a committee of the Dearborn Lodge (naming some order to which the householder actually belongs) to present Mr. Rahner with this beautiful sofa (indicating an imposing piece of furniture on the wagon). Shall my men bring it in?"

"Why, yes, if you are sure this is the right place."

"No mistake about that, Madam; Mr. Rahner is greatly esteemed by the members of the lodge and this gift is to be a complete surprise!"

So in the sofa is carried and deposited in a place of honor in the drawing-room. The polite "lodge member" depreciating all thanks departs and the team drives away.

A few hours later the polite stranger reappears in hot haste and the wagon drives up again. He is profuse in his apologies, but an error has been made.

"So unfortunate! So sorry to inconvenience you, but do you know I have made such a stupid blunder about the address—the sofa is to go to Brother John Rahner, of South Main Street, instead of North Main Street. Would it be too much bother to allow my men to enter and take it away? We are very anxious to deliver it before Brother Rahner returns, as it is a surprise for him!"

Of course, there is nothing to be done but let the beautiful sofa go, and, amid the apologies and excuses of the polite stranger, the sofa is again carried forth to the wagon and is driven away. The polite stranger also disappears, and, it is needless to say, is seen no more in that part of the town.

The next act on the program is the startling discovery that the house has been robbed of, perhaps, many thousands of dollars' worth of jewels and silver. How was it done?

The explanation is very simple. The sofa is specially

constructed with a hollow compartment of considerable size. Inside a girl has been concealed, who, when the sofa is left alone, quietly comes out and ransacks the place and retreats with her plunder into this convenient hiding-place. Girl, plunder, and sofa are then all carried away together and the thieves make good their escape without delay.

This is a new game, and, as I say, has been worked with many variations and usually with success in almost every city in England and on the continent.

RAPP: "I look upon you, sir, as a rascal!"

PARTEE: "You are privileged to look upon me in any character you desire to assume, sir."

"Did you ever go to a military ball?" asked a lisping maid of an army veteran.

"No, my dear," growled the old soldier, "but once I had a military ball come to me, and what do you think — it took my arm off!"

SHOT TWELVE

THERE are certain classes of men, and women, too, who, while not actually criminal, are yet so close to the boundary line in their practises as to need some special mention in this book. Take, for instance, the many so-called "divine" or mental healers, who pretend to cure all sorts of diseases by the laying on of hands or simply absent treatment, or the old-style patent medicine fraud who retailed sweetened and colored water under some high-sounding name, as Dr. So and So's Elixir and Tonic, from the tail-end of a cart, after having attracted a crowd of the curious with a lecture or open-air minstrel show.

"Far be if for me" to decry the actual healing and curative value of many excellent proprietary medicines and preparations on the market to-day. But among the good there are many that are worthless, and I should advise my readers to take such "remedies" only on the advice of their family physician.

The fake "doctor" is still with us, and his advertisements are often to be seen in the newspapers of America. They usually advertise under some honest-sounding name, and assume all the titles and learned degrees of two continents. Some are actually physicians, and, failing in the regular practise, have set out to make a living by deluding suffering humanity. It would be amusing, if it were not sorrowful, to see the crowds of patients who bring their ailments to such "doctors." The game is to give the sufferer some relief at first, in order to encourage him, and then prolong his case through many weary weeks and months, until they have gotten all the money he can afford to spend. Such doctors usually call themselves "specialists," but their real specialty is in exhorting money from their dupes, and my advice is to keep as far away from them as possible.

Thanks to the energetic efforts of the authorities many, if not all, of these practitioners have been driven out, and it is to be hoped that such tragedies as that unearthed in the Susan Geary case will be rare in the future.

The case of Francis Truth, alias Will Bemis, the self-styled Divine Healer, attracted no little attention throughout the East, especially in Boston, a few years ago. The man was a handsome, plausible, smooth-spoken man, who claimed to have some mysterious mesmeric power by which he could cure any disease, simply by the laying on of hands. His advertisements bristled with testimonials and brilliant promises, and he did a good business among the credulous. Many, who doubtless had nothing whatever the matter with them, were hypnotized into the belief that they were cured.

THE FAKE HEALER

Finally, Truth — or Bemis — found his money getting limited, because he could only "treat" a limited number a day. Then he had recourse to the absent-treatment dodge. He would tell his patients that he would give them an absent treatment at a certain hour, and at that time they were to retire to their rooms and think of him, and they would receive the healing influence! As the number of his dupes grew, he branched into a mail-order feature, until hundreds and thousands of people who had never seen the "healer" were sending him money by mail. He received hundreds of letters each day, until the post-office was forced to deliver them in great bags, and his income amounted to thousands of dollars a week! Truth lived in great style, drove about in his own carriage, had quite an office force of stenographers and clerks to handle the mail, and was getting rich, hand over fist, when the post-office authorities and the police put an end to his career.

Advertising mediums, clairvoyants, and astrologers have hosts of dupes, and some invite the methods of the confidence man, with mystical advice and fortune-telling. Not long ago, a certain Miss Ethel L——, of Malden, Mass., visited a so-called medium in Boston. As soon as she entered his inner sanctum she was surprised to have him caution her about a large sum of money which she was carrying. This "occult" knowledge so inspired her confidence, that she asked his advice about a suit she was interested in. He told her he would have to put her in a trance, which he did. When she came out of it, he cautioned her to go directly home, and to *hold her fingers crossed* until she reached her own room, where she must remain for two days. It was actually some hours before she realized that she had been robbed of $1,000 which she had in her pocket! Of course, the medium had disappeared!

I must say that with all its boasted culture and learning, Boston seems to be a favorite city for all sorts of schemes of this kind; astrologers, mediums, clairvoyants, test-mediums, and the like abound in the Hub as in few other places it has been my good fortune to visit, and I have been all over the world. Chicago also has its share.

New Yorkers pride themselves in believing in nothing at

all, and yet it was only a short time ago that a man named Ridgley, and calling himself the East Indian Mystery, victimized many people of wealth and fashion in that metropolis. This remarkable person combined the fakir of the East with the modern magnetic healer and the Voodo doctor of French Louisiana. The man himself is 70 years old. He is small, spry, alert, and wonderfully shrewd. His beard is bushy and black, except where age has whitened the edges, and grows thick and curly at the sides. The nose is as flat as a negro's. He denies negro blood, however, and abhors the race. He claims to be from Hindoostan, and talks to others in the house in a strange tongue.

THE "VOODO" DOCTOR

The eyes of the man are small, shrewd, and dark. The forehead, from each side of which grows gray, bushy hair that hides the ears, is high, receding, and intelligent.

"I knew you were coming," says this wizard-like man, "and I determined to receive you though warned against you. Now you want to know what I am, what I do. Let us be honest with each other."

He chooses big words as he proceeds to describe himself. They are used aptly, but mispronounced. The "th" becomes "d," and there are other things not unfamiliar in the Southern negro. The East Indian proceeds to read your character and to tell you of your life. He does it well.

"I am not a fortune-teller," he explains. "They are frauds, and I am a physiognomist. I read from the apex of the nose to the top of the forehead. I don't predict; I tell you; and I don't ask you to say if I am right or wrong."

It is said that among this man's patrons have been men and women whose names are a part of the life of New York.

It is also said that a recent marriage which astonished New York society came after the woman in the case had consulted this strange combination of charlatan and physician. She confided to him her desire, told him of her repeated failures to secure her wish, took the treatment, and in three months was married. Then followed, so the story goes, many presents, among them a tenement to the East Indian.

Spiritualism has many followers, and at one time I was almost a believer, but this was before I made a thorough investigation, which I have followed up even to the present day. I have never seen a materialization or a manifestation which I cannot fully explain. Of course, I cannot explain those that I "hear" about, as no two people see the same one thing alike.

Spiritualism is really a beautiful belief for those that are honest and believe in it; but as I have visited the greatest spiritualistic meetings in the world, I am sorry to say that no one has ever produced anything for me that would smack of the spiritual.

In Germany, spirit mediums are put in jail for obtaining money under false pretences. In England, Maskenlyne, of Maskenlyne & Cook, has done a great deal to keep the so-called fraud spiritualistic mediums out of England. In the future, I contemplate writing a book on spiritualistic methods, and how they do their tricks. I do not mean genuine spiritualists who have no tricks, but those mediums who use their knowledge of magic to gain a living.

The Davenport Brothers, during their short but strenuous career, had a terrible time of it in their journeys abroad. They were driven out of England, but they made enough money to last them the rest of their lives.

SHOT THIRTEEN

BOGUS TREASURES

NEVER believe that a so-called antique piece of furniture or a painting by one of the old masters is genuine until its authenticity has been proven beyond a possible doubt. That is my advice, and if you, reader, could see some of the impositions practised upon wealthy collectors and curio hunters, you, too, would take that view.

The people who purchase this class of goods are usually new-made millionaires, ambitious to own an art gallery of old masters. It would give them little satisfaction to know that some of their priceless treasures are simply copies, and often poor ones at that. M. Felix Duquesnel, of Paris, famous as an art critic, says that certain galleries of ancient masters contain few pictures more than ten years old. Forged pictures are regularly included in sales of private collections in which they never belonged. Nor is a written and duly attested pedigree of the least value. I know of one case in London where a dealer in fake antiques sought out an impoverished nobleman whose only property besides his title was an ancient manor house that was heavily mortgaged. The house was in a remote spot and had scarcely a stick of furniture left in it. The dealer bought it and sent out to it many vanloads of paintings, black oak furniture, arms, armour, moth-eaten tapestry, etc. In a few weeks he announced a sale of art treasures at the ancient home of the last of an ancient race. The sale actually lasted several

THE REDUCED NOBLEMAN

weeks as though the very cellars had been packed with "art treasures."

On the continent, to my certain knowledge, the case is even worse. One man that began life as a sculpture's assistant, but soon began the manufacture of imitations of "ancient" statues and "antique" furniture and now makes about $7,500 a year and employs several workmen.

His masterpieces are certain Greek heads "attributed to Phidias," but he also makes eighteenth century and Empire furniture. The opinion of such an authority is valuable. He says:

"You can take it as a fact that even an art expert can no longer tell if a piece of furniture is a forgery. At least, yes, he can tell if he takes the furniture to pieces. But few will dare incur that responsibility because you spoil the piece."

This cultivator of the artistic sense talks to his friends of one of the best-known Paris collectors, who bought at an enormous price an "eighteenth century" writing desk:

"He purchased with a written guarantee from a respectable dealer, who was in good faith. Well, this table comes from my own workroom, only if I told the owner he probably would not believe me."

A dealer who lives not far from the church of the Madeline in Paris keeps the choicest "fakes" in his bedroom. He never shows his private collection, as he calls it, until the wealthy amateur tearfully begs to see it. The gem of the collection is the dealer's own bed in Louis XVI. style.

He has sold his bed five or six times, but still sleeps well, I suppose because he "lies so easy," like a most honorable Frenchman.

At this moment, eighteenth-century engravings, including colored prints, are counterfeited on a vast scale.

Jewelry is made to look old by steeping in sulphuric acid for silver, or *aqua regia* for gold. The surface is worn with ground brick. The stones are then inserted and the whole is greased with tallow and rubbed in white soot.

Greek and Roman jewels, Renaissance enamels, Episcopal rings, and Benvenuto Cellini plate are "made in Germany."

Vienna is specialized in counterfeiting sixteenth-century enamels.

THE AUCTIONEER

Abbeville and Armiens make flint arrow-tops and hatchets for museums of geology.

Old pewters are manufactured at Roden. Etruscan pottery comes from Leeds.

In Holland, I met a student who was in demand as he could forge any of the old masters' signatures on oil paintings.

SHOT FOURTEEN

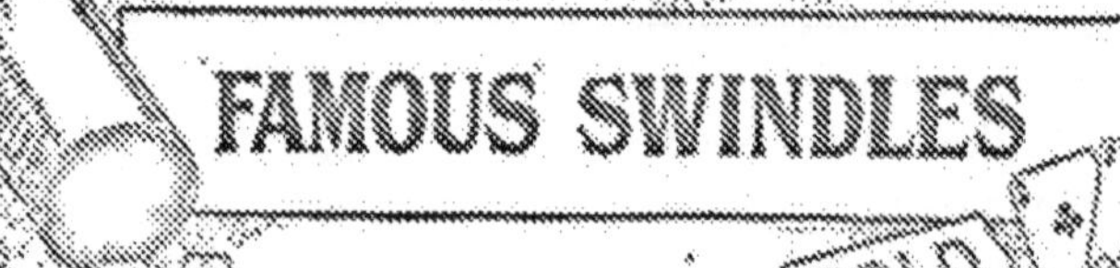

FOR years it has been a constant wonder to me how bare-faced swindling operations are carried on in almost open defiance of the laws of the land. There are a thousand-and-one-get-rich-quick schemes that each find their victims; it is needless to say that they bring wealth only to the promoter. There are more ways of swindling than with loaded dice and gold bricks.

Stock is sold in mining property where neither gold or silver ever existed, and the only metal about the proposition is the brazen cheek of the organizer of the company. Great promises of dividends are made, which are sometimes even paid out of the money received from the sale of the stock. Oil wells, gold mines, silver mines, and copper mines are exploited in this way to the great profit of the exploiter.

THE PROMOTER OF "FAKE" MONEY SCHEMES

A species of swindle that has been perpetrated times without number all over this country is the old gold-brick game. It does seem as though this had been exposed so frequently that the most ignorant countryman would know enough to keep away from any one who offers to sell an ingot or "brick" of pure gold at a sacrifice; but still there are pigeons to be plucked. The usual method is to meet a likely person and with great show of secrecy unfold the story of the poor Mexican miner who has a lump of pure gold valued at $5,000, which he will sell for $500 down! The pigeon comes fluttering, drawn by the tempting bait; meets the miner, sees the glittering brick, handles it, even tests it with acid, and, finally, is induced to put down his good money. With great show of secrecy and caution the brick is handled over and the victim departs only to learn later that "all is not gold that glitters" and that he is out his $500!

Much ingenuity is exercised in fixing up the "brick" so it will stand inspection. Sometimes even wedges of good gold are inserted in the cheap metal, and the operator saws or files into this wedge to take out gold for the victim to test. In these enlightened days, I do not need to tell you that all such stories, no matter how plausible, should be questioned and rejected at once.

The green-goods swindle is an elaborate game which begins with some very adroit correspondence in which the writer claims to be in possession of some old and discarded steel plates used in printing United States money, and for that

"FAKE" TEST OF GOLD BRICK

reason he is able to produce actual greenbacks which will pass anywhere. The letter usually begins something like this:

Dear Sir: — I am in possession of a good thing and with your confidential and friendly cooperation I can make you independently rich and at the same time better my own condition. . . . You will see that my goods are not what the law can class as real counterfeits, inasmuch as they are printed from genuine plates and can easily be passed in your section of the country.

The letter goes on to explain the necessity of a personal interview, offers to guarantee travelling expenses, and quotes prices usually as follows: $300 real money buys $3,000; $1,000 buys $30,000, etc. The pigeon is given a password and number with which he must sign all telegrams. Finally, not to go into too many details, the green goods operator and the victim meet with great secrecy — a package of real money is produced for inspection, the purchase money is paid over, and the package which has been deftly exchanged for another package containing worthless paper is given to the purchaser, who departs to learn his loss as soon as he opens his "bundle."

Of course, there is no redress possible. The whole game is a swindle. Never but once to the best of my knowledge have actual original plates been stolen from the government, and that was when Langdon W. Moore was able to use his influence with a gang of counterfeiters and secure the return of the 5–20 bond plate in the early 80's as described in Chapter XV. of his autobiography. Even if the plates were stolen as the green goods man pretends, the bills printed from them by unauthorized persons would be counterfeit in the eyes of the law.

Keep just as far away from any such scheme as you can.

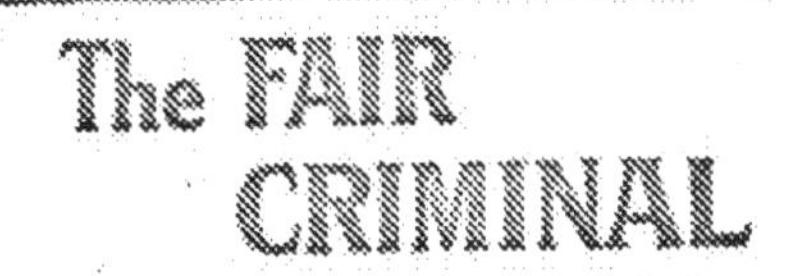

THERE have arisen in every country, and in every age, celebrated women criminals whose daring deeds have become part of history. From Lucrezia Borgia of the fifteenth century to Cassie Chadwick of the present day, the list is a long one, and yet police officials and prosecuting officers will no doubt agree with me, when I say that there are vastly fewer women criminals than men who lead dishonest lives.

The truth seems to be that when lovely woman stoops to crime, she usually goes to the greatest lengths of iniquity, and the comparatively few women who have perpetrated great crimes are made more conspicuous and more talked about by reason of their sex. In the United States, authorities claim that only one-tenth of persons accused of crime are women; while in France, Statistician Tarde declares that one-sixth is the usual proportion. Women criminals are certain to end their careers in wretchedness, if not in prison. Mothers of wayward girls are often much to blame for the beginning of careers of vice. A good home is the best protection, and upon every fair reader I urge the wisdom not only of choosing for herself the better way, but of safeguarding her sisters everywhere.

"Sophie" Lyons may be taken as a typical case of a born woman criminal. She came of a race of criminals. Her grandfather was a noted burglar in England, her father and mother, who came to America before she was born, both had a criminal record. She was taught to steal as soon as she could walk, and at twelve was arrested for shoplifting. At sixteen she was married to Maury Harris, a pickpocket, but her husband was sentenced to two years in State prison before the honeymoon was over. Later she married "Ned" Lyons, the noted burglar, and became one of the most expert female pickpockets in the country.

"Sophie" Lyons was a beautiful girl with brilliant dark eyes, abundant auburn hair, and a fascinating manner. At the county fairs she would make the acquaintance of men of wealth, and deftly relieve them of their watch or roll of banknotes, while they were fascinated with her blandishments. If caught, she was a consummate actress, and could counterfeit every shade of emotion. Real tears of injured innocence would flow from her beautiful eyes. Lyons pulled off a big coup about two years after their marriage, bought a villa on Long Island with the proceeds, and, though a professional burglar himself, tried to keep his wife from stealing. The taint was too strong, however; she picked pockets for the love of it. Eventually, both husband and wife were sentenced to Sing Sing Prison, from which they make a sensational escape and got away to Paris. In France, under the name of Madame d' Varney, she continued her brilliant career of crime. Sophie

THE "CONFIDENCE QUEEN" AT WORK

Lyons is supposed to be at large at the present time—somewhere in America. She has one son serving a term in State prison, and two daughters who are being carefully educated in Germany, kept as far as possible in ignorance of their mother's actual character.

The career of Cassie Chadwick, the "Duchess of Diamonds" is of more recent date. She is a woman of about fifty years of age, and has neither great physical beauty or great personal charm, yet she must have had wonderful powers of persuasion, for she victimized such men as Andrew Carnegie, and made Banker Ira Reynolds believe she was an illegitimate child of the Scotch millionaire. With him she deposited a bundle of securities alleged to be worth $5,000,000 and a note for half a million dollars bearing Carnegie's signature. A signed paper from Reynolds attesting the fact that he held $5,000,000 worth of securities in trust for her became her stock in trade, and she fleeced bankers and business men to the tune of one million dollars in money, and $150,000 worth of jewels in four years. In March, 1905, she was convicted, and is now serving a ten-year sentence in the Ohio State penitentiary. Thanksgiving, 1905, during my engagement at Keith's Theatre, I gave a performance for the prisoners in the county jail in Cleveland, and Mrs. Chadwick was to be entertained in her cell; but fifteen minutes before I was to show her a few conjuring tricks, she changed her mood, gave the jailer an argument, and refused to allow any one near her cell.

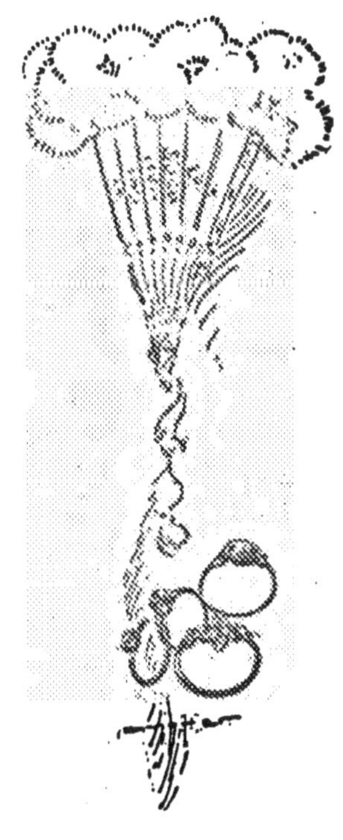

Of the army of women shoplifters, petty thieves, stool-pigeons for confidence men, etc., little need be said. Shoplifting seems to be the most common crime. Many women steal for mere wantonness, having no need of the articles or money. Kleptomania is a polite word for this offense, and, doubtless, there are cases of mental disorder and moral degeneracy which takes this form.

The time-worn badger game, as it is called, is still frequently employed to fleece men. The confidence woman gets acquainted with some man of means, preferably a married man of family, and invites him to call at her apartments. She carries on her part of the flirtation to "*perfection*" till suddenly the doorbell rings, and in apparent fright she exclaims: "There comes my husband. He is furiously jealous and will kill you!"

The fictitious husband rushes in, a scene takes place, and the "husband" threatens to shoot or call in the police. Eventually, the matter is settled by the victim giving up a large sum of money rather than face a scandal. This is only one form of blackmail resorted to, to extort money, as the victim is often threatened with public exposé, etc. Pirates in petticoats frequently ply their trade on ocean and lake steamers. They are well-dressed and ingratiate themselves with the passengers of both sexes, watching their opportunity to steal jewelry, or practise their threadbare confidence games.

A woman named Grace Mordaunt cleared many thousands of dollars in New York by occasionally advertising the following personal in the *Herald:* "Young widow, financially embarrassed wishes loan of $100 on a diamond ring worth twice as much. Address Box ——."

Miss Mordaunt was beautiful and fascinating. She would produce a genuine diamond ring, and go with her victim to a jeweler to have it priced. At his office she would receive her money, and ask him with tears not to wear or show her ring for a few days, but lock it up in his safe. She then takes the ring, wraps it up in tissue paper, puts it in an envelope, and hands it sealed to the victim, and leaves, promising to repay the money with interest in a few days. She never returns, and at length the victim opens the envelope to find a brass ring with a glass diamond worth about 25 cents.

While in Austria some years ago, I heard of a most remarkable adventuress who went under the name of Madame Clarice B——. Her particular form of swindle was to get acquainted with young men of good family and wealth, and entangle them in her meshes, and get declarations of marriage from them. She would get all she could out of her poor dupe, and then notify the family of the "engagement." The young man's parents would then be forced to buy her off with a large sum of money, when she would go to pastures new. But Madame Clarice met her Waterloo in Vienna. There she met an American student upon whom she worked her wiles even to the extent of going through a marriage ceremony with him. After a time she left him and went to Paris, but the adventuress who had broken so many hearts found her own touched at last. She was actually in love with her student husband whose face haunted her dreams. After a few days she returned to Vienna, sought him out, and confessed all, but through herself on his mercy and love. The denouncement, unusual in such cases, was that the couple were actually married, and to-day are living happily on the continent.

Many, many more incidents might be related of the clever work of the facinating woman criminal, but these should be sufficient to warn the unwary against trusting either their honor or their pocketbook to an unknown woman no matter how beautiful.

⚜ ⚜ ⚜

TEACHER (instructing prisoner class on manners): "Now, Willie Brown, for example, if you were sitting in an electric car, every seat occupied, and an old lady enters, what would you do?"

TOMMY: "Please, sir, I would pretend I was sleepin'.

SHOT SIXTEEN

The "BRACE" GAME

F all classes of criminals the professional gambler has probably played the most conspicuous part in fiction and melodrama. We all know the stage gambler, while the penny dreadful novels and story-books are too often filled with descriptions of this kind of crime. The gambler of the stage and in the novel is but an exaggerated portrait of this type.

Gambling is the playing for money of games depending solely on chance, like roulette; or games of skill and chance like poker and other card games or billiards and the like. A gentleman may have the moral right to back his own opinion in a wager with money, and with true sportsman instinct stand success or defeat. Even a small stake at cards is dangerous, for it cultivates the habit of gambling, which may soon become a passion.

Gambling in itself is bad enough even when the game is square; but your professional gambler never plays the game that way. He is an expert with cards. His seemingly innocent shuffle of the pack gives him a full knowledge of where every card is located. He deals you a hand good enough to induce you to make dangerously high bets, but not high enough to win. He lures his victim by small winnings to destruction in the end. He uses cards so cleverly marked on the back that he can read the values of your hand as well as if he were looking over your shoulder, and govern his play accordingly. In faro and roulette he uses mechanical devices for controlling absolutely the winning numbers, and so cheats his victim from beginning to end. When a gambler employs a fraudulent deck of cards or a cheating-roulette wheel or faro-box it is called a "brace" game. No novice can go up against a brace game with any hope of winning; he must lose. Even if the game were on the square the victim will invariably lose in the long run, for the percentage of chance is against him. If the exposures, which I feel at liberty to make in this chapter, may warn the unwary and deter the youth of this land from the fascinations of the green cloth, I shall feel that my efforts have not been in vain.

A "BRACE" SPINDLE

Marked cards employed by gamblers are specially engraved packs of cards in which the usual decoration design of scrolls and flowers on the back, instead of being exactly identical on the fifty-two cards, is varied slightly for each of the high cards. This would not be noticed and cannot be detected without close examination, but it renders the back of the cards as legible to the gambler as the face. The turn of a leaf in the scroll work may mean that that card is the ace of diamonds, while a slightly different turn may mean the ace of hearts and so on.

With such a pack of cards the gambler has the poor dupe at his mercy. "Long cards" and strippers, as they are called, are special packs in which the high cards are slightly different in shape and width, enabling the gambler, for instance, with a single motion to take three of the aces out of a pack.

The hold out, as it is called, is a mechanical contrivance used for holding a card fraudulently withdrawn from the pack until it is wanted. The hold out, illustrated in this chapter, I purchased from a notorious gambler who has now retired, and perfected it for use in certain card tricks. I have found, however, that certain professional gamblers have got hold of it, and I shall therefore expose its operations so that the unwary may be warned. The machine is adjusted to the arm inside the coat sleeve. The mechanism is

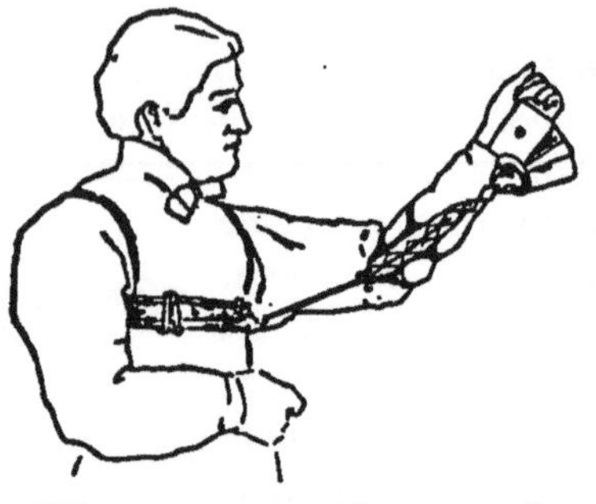

THE ARM AND CHEST "HOLD OUT"

worked by a band passing around the chest. By taking a long breath the machine is made to move and pushes its mechanical fingers down inside the sleeve to the hand. As the breath is exhaled the "fingers" go back in the sleeve, taking with them the card or cards the gambler wishes to hold out. The same operation causes the cards to be returned to the hand. It is as though the gambler were gifted with a third and invisible arm and hand; it cannot be detected in operation.

Other hold outs are attached under the table. One called the "Goose neck" is brazenly advertised in a certain catalogue I have on my desk as I write, and the price is $15. This, I quote from the catalogue, "is worked by the knee or foot, making the cards come up over the edges of the table into the hand." A "vest hold out" is made and sold, vest and all, for $30; and a new "cold deck" hold out for substituting an entirely different pack of cards which has been previously stacked for $35. Concerning this latter contrivance, the manufacturer says: "Made to hold a full deck. Cards can be arranged to suit you, and when opportunity presents itself make the switch and you can clean up everything in sight."

A mere list of the fraudulent contrivances for cheating at gambling should be sufficient to prevent any honest man from ever going up against a gambler's game, The Lucus spindle, as it is called, is apparently a very simple contrivance which the novice thinks must certainly be on the square. As a matter of fact, it is fraudulent and made with that intention. Its makers claim that it can actually be handed to an officer for exami-

THE "SQUEEZE" SPINDLE

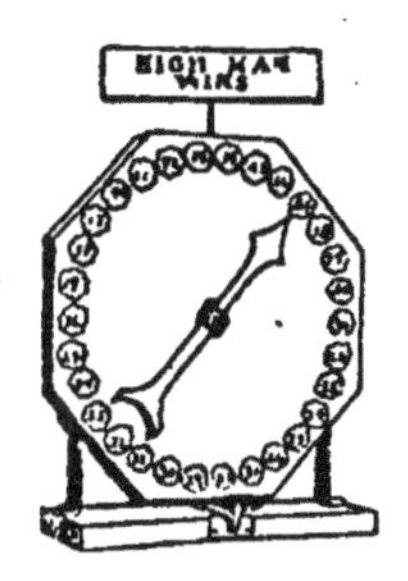

A CHEATING DEVICE

nation without detection. The old "Simplicity Squeeze Spindle" works on a different principle, but is just as effective. It is under control of the gambler and can be stopped on whatever figure will win him the most money. The "High Man Wins" arrow is for use in barrooms and is a brace game, the house being a large winner.

One of the most malicious little devices I have ever run across is sometimes called a vest-pock roulette wheel. It would seem that this must be square and that the player would have even a greater chance to win than on an ordinary wheel because there is only one zero. As a matter of fact, however, it is a fraud pure and simple, as the mechanism is so arranged that the pointer will stop on zero three times when it will stop on any other number once! So beware of the man with a little Monte Carlo in his pocket.

Among other things used by professional gamblers to cheat with are loaded dice which may be bought or made to order; adhesive palming cloth for palming cards, chips, dice, etc.; adhesive dice which almost defy detection; shaped dice which are not exact cubes; "brace" dice boxes; magnifying mirrors set in rings; shading boxes made to sew on inside of coat and used to shade or mark cards while the game is in progress; marked decks of cards, ring hold outs, bouncers for roulette wheels, cement for plugging dice, silver amalgam for loading dice, "brace" faro boxes, etc., etc.

With such an equipment, united with years of experience and skill, what chance has any law-abiding citizen against the professional gambler? The reader does not need my secret of escaping from handcuffs to shake off the shackles of this alluring siren gambling.

POCKET ROULETTE

SHOT SEVENTEEN

CHEATING UNCLE SAM

UNDER this heading I shall group such crimes as counterfeiting and the kindred crimes of forgery and raising notes, as well as smuggling. It is a serious matter to get into trouble with the Federal government. The criminal is pursued relentlessly, and the sentence when conviction follows the almost certain arrest is always a heavy one. For these reasons such crimes are usually attempted only by the boldest and most skilful criminals or by those whose positions of trust in government employ afford them special opportunities.

The three great crimes against any government (aside, of course, from actual treason) are counterfeiting its money, either gold, silver, or bills; evading its custom laws, or smuggling. Counterfeiting, which offers enormous rewards if successful, is frequently attempted — indeed, scarcely a month passes that does not see the appearance of some new and

THE FORGER AT WORK

dangerous counterfeit of some United States bill. Notice is at once sent to all the banks by the authorities and often published in the newspapers, so that the public at large may be warned against the spurious bill in circulation.

Many years ago, when the art of engraving and plate making was in its infancy, the paper money in circulation was much more crude than to-day. Then it was comparatively easy for the counterfeiter to engrave just as good a bill as the government could produce; but now the matter is much more difficult, owing to the delicate and intricate work of the lathe and tool work and the special fibre paper upon which it is printed. The conditions of caution surrounding the government printing works make it almost impossible for an original plate to be stolen. The paper is made especially for this purpose and under strictest government supervision. In designing, lettering, and engraving the bills only artists of the foremost professional standing are employed. Every banknote or greenback is truly a work of art, so that an exact counterfeit — one that will deceive even an ordinary business man accustomed to handle money — is each year more and more difficult to produce.

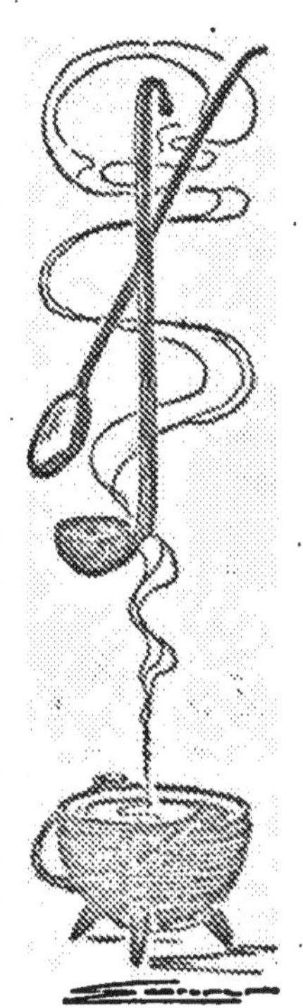

The counterfeits of silver and gold coins are mostly of two kinds — either moulded or stamped with a die. The die-made counterfeits are usually much more difficult to detect if the metal employed has anywhere near the right weight, ring, and color. Electroplating is employed by counterfeiters with some success; one dangerous counterfeit now in circulation is a compound of antimony and lead heavily electroplated with silver. In this way the gold ten-dollar piece of 1858 and the gold five-dollar pieces of 1847, 1848, 1862, and 1869 have been counterfeited with a platinum coin heavily gold plated. The most successful and, therefore, the most dangerous of all counterfeits are those composed of actual gold and silver but with a mixture of metal. The actual value of the gold in the counterfeit five-dollar gold pieces dated 1881 and 1882 has been determined by assay to be $4.43.

Genuine gold and silver coins are often tampered with. These schemes are known as "sweating," "plugging," and "filling." For instance, a hundred gold ten-dollar pieces subject to an acid bath would lose perhaps $35 or $40 worth of their gold and remain unchanged in appearance. The coins are put in circulation again, and the gold which has been "sweated" off of them is easily extracted from the acid bath and sold. Coins are also robbed of precious metal by drilling a hole, the cavity being filled with an alloy and the filling covered with a light gold wash. Filling a coin is sawing it through the edge in two parts, scraping out the gold, and putting the two parts together again filled with some baser metal. Thomas Ballard was the first counterfeiter to successfully reproduce government fibre paper, which he did in 1870. The next year he and his gang were captured, but escaped from jail and found a hiding-place from which they continued to issue dangerous counterfeits. In 1873 his counterfeit $500 treasury note alarmed banks and government officials. Ballard was finally captured in his lair in Buffalo just as he was about to produce a counterfeit $5 bill of a Canadian bank. This bill, he boasted, was to have corrupted all Canada.

John Peter McCartney was the counterfeiter who successfully removed all the ink from genuine $1 bills so that he could secure government paper on which to print counterfeit bills of much higher denomination. He made a fortune, so it is said, but was brought to book at last.

To a counterfeiter named "One-eyed Thompson" is given the credit of being the first to transform bills of small denomination to larger by cutting and pasting. He also had an ingenious trick of cutting up $10 or $100 bills into strips and making eleven counterfeit bills of the same denomination.

A German by the name of Charles Ulrich won the distinction of having produced the most dangerous Bank of England notes ever made.

Langdon W. Moore, one time expert bank robber, forger, and counterfeiter, who has now reformed and is leading an honest life, has written an interesting autobiography in which he tells of his own experience in raising notes, counterfeiting, and getting the counterfeits in circulation. At one time another gang of counterfeiters declared war on him. He sent a spy into the enemy's camp, learned where they were going to put out their next batch of "queer," and then proceeded to carry out a plan for outwitting them.

Postage stamp counterfeits are common enough, but mostly practised to impose on the collectors of rare stamps: for instance, a certain issue of Hawaiian stamps are very valuable as there are not supposed to be more than half a dozen or so in existence, and when one is found it sells for thousands of dollars. One of the most daring stamp counterfeiters "planted" about twenty forgeries of this rare stamp into collections of wealthy philatelists and realized many thousands of dollars.

Another daring gang introduced a beautifully-engraved stamp into Paris by posing as the "King of Sodang" and suite — Sodang being an island that existed solely in the imagination of the clever swindler. A stamp dealer was the principal victim and paid the "king" a large sum of money for a number of the stamps of this fictitious kingdom.

Speaking of stamps recalls a method of secret writing which defied detection. The plan was to put a fake letter inside the envelope, but to write the real message in microscopic characters in the upper right-hand corner, and over this paste the stamp. The correspondent, who was, of course, in the secret, would simply soak off the stamp.

A PRISONER'S SECRET MESSAGE

This trick is often made use of by convicts who wish to send a secret message to their friends on the outside.

Cancelled postage stamps are frequently washed and sold or used again. I have in my possession a receipt given me by a Russian convict which will do this perfectly, removing every trace of the cancellation mark, but leaving the stamp perfect. Such a secret is too dangerous, however, for general publication.

On the continent I have known of a clever dodge being practised which reaches the same result. Before the letter is mailed the stamp is covered with a transparent paste. When the letter is received the correspondent can simply wash off the stamp with water, and, of course, the cancellation marks with it. The penalty for this crime is so severe, and the reward so small, that not even hardened criminals are willing to risk the attempt.

A clever gang of smugglers adopted this ruse in order to get their trunks through the custom-house free. They had counterfeit labels made, such as an inspector places upon a trunk. Passing among the trunks where the inspectors were at work they would slyly poke the "inspected" label on all their own trunks. Each official seeing the labels would suppose some other official had actually inspected the trunks and so would pass on to others.

Instances might be multiplied, but all goes to show that dishonesty, whether to your fellowmen or to the government, is the worst of all policies in the end.

SHOT EIGHTEEN

A HUMBUG or a hoax is often comparatively harmless in its nature — more in the way of a high practical joke upon the public. Long ago P. T. Barnum, the great American showman, declared: "The American people want to be humbugged." I believe he was right and certainly his great success in the show business would seem to point to the same conclusion. In my own particular work I find there is so much that is marvellous and wonderful that can be accomplished by perfectly natural means that I have no need to find recourse to humbugging the public. In my case, at least, truth is stranger than fiction.

At the present day a firm in New York makes a business of manufacturing fakes like double-bodied babies, mermaids, and fake mummies. Dr. L. D. Weiss, of New York, discovered that he could detect a fake mummy from an original by placing it under his X-Ray machine.

Another clever hoax which created much amusement at the time was contrived by some English students years ago and perpetrated at a county fair. On a vacant lot near the fair a large tent was erected and a huge placard announced that "The Great Wusser" was on exhibition within — admission free! It was supposed that some payment or purchase would be required inside, but it was not so. The crowd, eager for free amusement, was formed into a long "queue," and the people — admitted only one at a time —

THE GREAT WUSSER

were escorted through a maze of hurdles into a darkened compartment of the tent before a curtain. There they were entreated not to irritate or disturb the "animal" in any way, and the curtain went up, disclosing a sorry and spavined looking donkey.

"This is the great Wusser," explained the showman. And when the bewildered spectator asked what it meant, he was told that, "though you may have seen as bad a donkey, you certainly never saw a wusser!" Then, when the victim of the hoax became indignant, he was besought to "keep it quiet" and take his revenge by allowing the remainder of the crowd to be hoaxed. This request showed a deep knowledge of human nature, for the victim always complied, and many went among the crowd and spread the most astonishing accounts of the "Great Wusser," and waited to see their comrades taken in. Eventually, however, rioting arose, and the jesters, being arrested for creating a disturbance, had to pay over $100 in fines and damages.

But humbugs are not all so harmless. An adroit rascal was caught not long ago in London who was posing as an American bishop. He was certainly a great humbug, for he looked the part of the "bishop" to perfection. It seems that he called in his carriage, mind you, at a well-known jewelers and asked to see some bracelets, mentioning that he was returning to America and wished to take a present to his wife. "Nothing very expensive," he said — "I could not afford that — but something about seventy or eighty pounds." Eventually, he agreed to take a bracelet that cost one hundred pounds. He said he would pay for it with a hundred pound note which he had with him. It was the only money he had with him at the moment, but he would wait while they sent it to the bank to ascertain that it was all right. He should really prefer doing this. They sent it to the bank and received answer that it was perfectly correct.

Having paid for his bracelet the bishop took it and was just about to step into his carriage when a policeman tapped him on the shoulder, and said, "Hellow Jim! You're up to your old tricks again, are you? You just come along with me;" and he took him back into the shop.

THE "BISHOP"

The jeweler said there was some mistake, that the gentleman was an American bishop, that he had bought a bracelet, and paid for it with an excellent note.

"Just let me look at the note, will you?" said the policeman. He looked at it, and said, "yes, it's just as I thought. This note is one of a particularly clever batch of forgeries which are very difficult to detect, and the man is no more a bishop than you are. We will go off to the police station at once. I will take the note and go on with the prisoner in advance, and you must send your salesman to me and meet us and bear witness." So the policeman took the bishop and the bracelet and the note, but when the jeweler's man reached the police station they had not arrived, and they have never been heard of since!

❦ ❦ ❦

Warden to new arrival, who happens to be enjoying the name of Moses Ikenstein:

"Well, Mr. Ikenstein, as this is your first visit it is our rule to always allow prisoners to select their own workshop, and if you will tell me what your trade or profession is will put you in that branch of employment."

IKENSTEIN: "Is that so? Well, I am a traveling salesman."

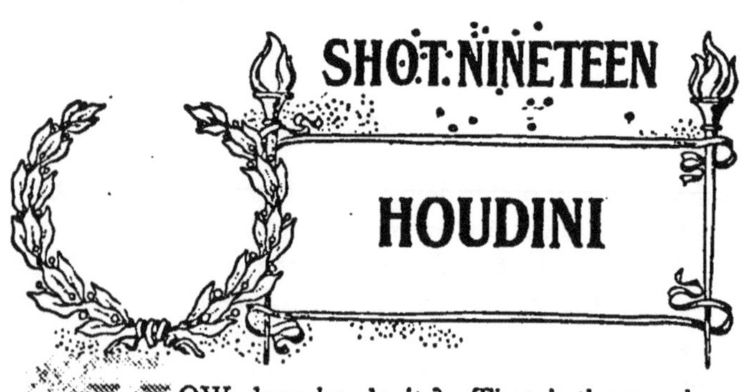

HOW does he do it? That is the usual question I hear asked about my work in the theater. No, dear reader, it is not my purpose to tell you *how* I open locks, *how* I escape from a prison cell into which I have been locked, having previously been stripped naked and manacled with heavy irons. I do not intend to tell you in this book *how* I escape from the trunk or the tightly corded and nailed-up box in which I have been confined, or *how* I unlock any regulation handcuff that can be produced — not yet.

Some day I may tell all this, and then you will know. At present, I prefer that all who see me should draw their own conclusions. But exactly how I accomplish these things I shall still leave you to guess, gentle reader. I should not want you to go into the show business. It's a hard life, "so they say."

"Have you ever been stuck at it?" I think I hear you ask. Not yet. I have had some pretty close calls, but have always pulled through somehow. The nearest I ever came to giving in was during my engagement at Blackbourne, England. There I offered a prize to the man who could fasten me in such a way that I could not escape. One man accepted my challenge. He was an instructor in athletics, and was out for blood. He evidently looked upon my challenge as a personal affront to him. At any rate, he started in to shackle me.

He first handcuffed my hands in front, then locked elbow

irons, the chain of which went behind my back. Then he handcuffed my legs, and after this bent me backward and chained my back and feet together. I had to kneel down. Every chain and handcuff was fitted to the limit. I started in, but at the end of an hour I suffered so under the strain that I asked to be let out. My back was aching, my circulation was stopped in my wrists, and my arms became paralyzed. My opponent's only reply was, "This is a bet. Cry quits or keep on."

The Music Hall where I was playing was packed, and while watching me became fairly wild. I kept on, but I was only about half conscious. Every joint in my body was aching, and I had but little use of my arms. I asked as a favor that he free my hands long enough for the circulation to start again, but he only laughed and exclaimed, "This is no love affair, this is a contest. Say you are defeated and I'll release you."

I gritted my teeth and went at it once more. For two hours and a half I exerted myself, fighting for my professional good name. In the meanwhile, the audience was cheering itself hoarse. Some cried "Give it up," and others, "Keep on, you'll do it." I don't believe any such scene was ever acted in a theater. The house was crazy with excitement, and I was covered with blood brought on by my exertion to release myself and chaffing irons. But I did it. I got free of every chain and handcuff. Then they had to carry me off the stage, and I suffered from the effects for months afterwards.

As for the prison cell, I have never been locked in one I could not open. I have had the honor of making my escape from securely locked cells in jails, prisons, and police stations in almost every large city in the world, and under the most rigid conditions. The chiefs of police, the wardens, the jailers, the detectives, and citizens who have been present at these tests know that they are real and actual. Perhaps the most historic American feat that gained for me the most notoriety was my escape January, 1906, from Cell 2, Murderers' Row, in the United States Jail at Washington, D. C.; from the very cell in which Guiteau, the assassin of President Garfield, was confined until he was led forth to be hanged. Since my return from abroad, October, 1905, I have escaped after being locked up in a nude state from cells in New York City, Brooklyn, Detroit, Rochester, Buffalo, Washington, Baltimore, Philadelphia, Providence, and City Tombs in Boston and Lowell. In all cases I submitted to a close search, being stark naked and heavily manacled into the cell, which was also thoroughly searched.

I am an American by birth, born in Appleton, Wis., U. S. A., on April 6, 1873. To my lot has fallen more experiences, more strange adventures, more ups and downs, in my thirty-three years of life than to most men.

When about nine years of age my mother, to whom I am greatly attached, apprenticed me to a mechanic to learn that trade; but, after an uneventful term with the tools of the trade, I resolved to see the world with my own eager eyes. So I ran away from home, and in this way made an early acquaintance with the corrugated side of life.

I joined a small circus, and soon learned to conduct the Punch and Judy show, to do a ventriloquial act, and to play town clown on the bars — "gol darn it." I also doubled in brass — that is, I beat the cymbals. I here gained the experiences that possibly ripened me into the world's Handcuff King and Prison Breaker — a title which I have justly earned.

But there was a time when I was not recognized as I am now. Those were the days of small things. That was in the middle West. After that, London and an engagement at the Alhambra. After that, everywhere on the continent and all over America. I have not yet been to Australia. I do not wish to be so far away from my mother.

While touring Germany I brought suit against the police

and a newspaper because they said my act was not genuine. I won the case — to have lost it would have meant ruin.

Again, in Russia, I was bound by the officials of the spy police and locked in a Siberian transport cell. Had I failed to escape, I would have been compelled to journey to Siberia, as the key that locks these cells does not open them. The governor-general in Siberia has the only key to open them. I was out in twenty minutes.

If there were more room in this book I would like to tell you of the many places in which I have played, both in America and Europe. I have many certificates from police officials. I was almost too busy to write this book, although I have been collecting the material for a long time. But now I am pleased it is written, and trust it may please you. I believe that the reading of this book will so familiarize the public with the methods of the criminal classes that it will enable law-abiding citizens to protect themselves from the snares of the evil-doer.

I hope it will warn you away from crime and all evil-doing. It may tell the "Right Way to Do Wrong," but, as I said in the beginning, all I have to say is "Don't."

Medal illustrated is the result of my winning the contest from the H. Siegel Company, expert packers. And Mr. B. F. Keith, by the way, also presented me with a most magnificent and costly Tiffany timepiece during my engagement in Boston.

Sincerely yours,

HARRY HOUDINI.

CONCLUSION

A CERTAIN fascination without doubt lingers about crime and the methods of criminals. Much of this fascination, and, consequently, much of the temptation to do wrong, arises from ignorance of the subject — ignorance of the mean, sordid life and the disgrace and punishment which are the certain result of a career of crime.

The wayward youth sees only the advantage to be gained by unlawful acts. He does not see the years of ignominy, the furtive hiding from the law, the shame of not being able to look his fellow-man in the face — no, nor the inevitable arrest, conviction, and punishment which ends it all in ninety-nine cases out of every one hundred.

In this book I have told of the methods of criminals, and held them up to your gaze, not as heroes, but as malefactors; not as examples to be emulated, but as corruptions to be shunned, as you would shun a plague.

To the best of my belief, this book, if you read it rightly, is a sermon more powerful against wrong-doing than many that are preached from the pulpit. It is my hope and wish that it may carry this warning into the hearts of thousands of young men. Then shall my labor not have been lost.

Lightning Source UK Ltd.
Milton Keynes UK
UKHW040638180521
383923UK00001B/103